Do the Right Thing

Do the Right Thing

*Real Life Stories of Leaders
Facing Tough Choices*

Stories from

Graduates of
Leaders for Global Operations
Massachusetts Institute of Technology

Edited by

Stephen Cook, Ruthie Davis, Dan Shockley, Jon Strimling, and Jeff Wilke

Manufacturing by CreateSpace
ISBN: 1502859882
ISBN 13: 9781502859884
Library of Congress Control Number: 2014922192
CreateSpace Independent Publishing Platform
North Charleston, South Carolina

Contents

You don't have a choice: it is your destiny to be a leader.
What's up to you is how effective you will be...

Don Davis

D id you know that you have the potential to be the kind of leader that people look up to, admire, and follow?

What if this book could give you a straightforward path to achieving that goal, honed over decades of intensive work and proven in the real-world experience of hundreds of business leaders?

This book itself is evidence of the strength of this path. The book was started by Don Davis, who led The Stanley Works for over two decades, and then taught leadership at MIT's Leaders for Global Operations program (LGO) for another twenty-six years. After Don passed away with this work unfinished, we, his students who found his lessons so inspirational and compelling, committed ourselves to carry forward his vision from concept to completion.

You can be the kind of leader that Don Davis was—authentic in everything you do and an inspiration to those around you. Don's mantras for effective leadership are illustrated here in the real-life stories of his students, who have gone on to lead some of the most sophisticated operations in the world. Don's lessons are presented in the way he shared them with us, using real-world stories to provoke thought, discussion, and personal growth.

We are very fortunate to have met Don and had him share his lessons with us directly. Our sole purpose for writing this book is to carry on Don's vision of sharing these timeless lessons. All proceeds from the sale of this book are dedicated to the pursuit of that cause.

Stephen Cook, Ruthie Davis, Dan Shockley,
Jon Strimling, and Jeff Wilke

Dedications

To my children and grandchildren, along with my five hundred students now part of corporate America, I dedicate this book.

This was the original dedication written by Don Davis.

This book is dedicated to Don Davis and to his hope that by reading it, you will become a better leader. We trust you will find Don's lessons as timeless and valuable as we have.

Don's daughter Ruthie, and students, Stephen, Dan, Jon, and Jeff

Foreword

By Ruthie Davis

My father planned to write this book. His working title was "Leaders Don't Choose Their Followers: Followers Choose Their Leaders." These are his notes for the foreword:

Foreword

This book is based on a lifetime of leadership experiences, capped by twenty years as CEO of The Stanley Works and twenty years teaching leadership and ethics at MIT. Adding richly to my career learnings have been my close relationships with my six children and twelve grandchildren. Further testing and tempering of my leadership convictions (i.e., mantras) have been provided by approximately five hundred dual-degree graduate students from MIT's Leaders for Manufacturing program.

My father's father was a teacher. He was a professor of journalism and head of the department at Penn State University. A humble man, he never broadcast his induction into the Advertising Hall of Fame. My father majored in journalism at Penn State before joining the navy in World War II and then graduating with an MBA from Harvard Business School.

His first company interview was with Stanley Tools. He was the last interview of the day, and the interviewer seemed tired and distracted. This didn't sit well with my father, so he showed up at the Stanley executive's hotel early the next morning. He waited in the lobby until the gentleman appeared on his way for breakfast. He approached him very politely and voiced his concern that his interview had not shown his full potential due to being last in a long line of interviews. The executive agreed to reinterview my father after breakfast.

He earned the position at Stanley and started a forty-five-year career with the company. He was a good communicator and a natural teacher and could connect with people. His first key position was VP of industrial relations. That was back in the heyday of organized labor, and he handled all negotiations with unions. He worked his way up the corporate ladder to spend twenty-one years as CEO, one of the longest tenures of a Fortune 500 CEO at one company.

The youngest of his six children, I essentially grew up with a CEO for a father. From an early age, I knew my father was a natural leader. I also knew he wasn't like other successful businessmen. He never had a luxury car or expensive watches or gadgets. He didn't want a parking spot at Stanley like the other executives, and he didn't want to live in the suburbs near the corporate headquarters, where most of the executives preferred to live. He chose to live in the working-class town where the Stanley factories were located. They still had factories in New Britain, Connecticut, and he wanted to have the same mayor, taxes, and library as the people who worked at Stanley making tools.

He believed in stewardship and that it was his duty to be involved with the town where he lived and worked. He served on boards of the local hospital, the Boys & Girls Club, New Britain public schools, and the New Britain Museum of American Art and was involved with numerous other institutions. My mother, Jinny Davis, was also heavily involved and volunteered within the community.

As a kid, I was aware of what my parents gave of themselves to others and was proud of it.

In some ways my father was very CEO-like at home. There were six kids, and it was like running a small company. You just always knew by the way he operated that he was a CEO. When we'd go skiing, we'd pile into the car Friday evening, and then at 6:00 a.m. the next morning in Vermont, he'd be making pancakes and oatmeal, and he'd line us up on the barstools in shifts. We had to get to the slopes by a certain time. It was somewhat of a regimen. There were lists. He was super activity oriented, and this never changed. Even later, when we visited my parents as adults, there was a schedule: we're going fishing at 6:00 a.m., we're having a lobster bake at five o'clock, we're gardening, we're doing this, we're doing that. My husband and my dad actually bonded over doing yard work at my parents' home on Martha's Vineyard.

But it was more than being superorganized. He and my mother raised us around certain strong beliefs at home, just as he taught leadership based on principles or what he called mantras. For example, take the dinner table at the Davis house. When someone did something wrong in my family, including either of my parents, that person would have to say out loud in front of the whole group, "I was wrong again," with the operative word being "again." Being wrong wasn't the issue, it was learning from it that mattered.

If someone tattled on a sibling in my house, the tattletale was the one who was in trouble with my mother and father. They did not like a snitch.

My parents let it be known that they didn't like spoiled kids. This meant we always had summer jobs, not too many perks like stereos, and we all wore older siblings' hand-me-downs. When I wanted to spend one summer at age sixteen playing the tournaments in the New England tennis circuit, I was informed that my parents would pay my tournament entry fees but that I would have to take care of all of the applications and find transportation to the events—even if that meant taking the bus. Why should Don and Jinny give up their summer carting me around to tournaments? They were the opposite of "little-league" parents.

On the other hand, I was often taken out of school to travel with my parents on business trips around the world—sleeping on the couch in their hotel room. They knew my education would not suffer from some global travel.

We were always encouraged to practice leadership. It was a skill that could be learned. I was encouraged to try to be team captain or serve on the student council or lead school projects. I was also taught to create leadership opportunities, which was the start of my many entrepreneurial ventures that began with selling golf balls and lemonade at age ten and went on to starting a tennis program at age thirteen and a summer housecleaning company at age sixteen.

At many of my sporting events and matches, I would see my CEO father on the sidelines in his work suit. He was not as concerned with my winning as with my sportsmanship on the field. His presence meant everything to me.

Since I didn't have a younger sibling, my parents felt it was important that I learn to be a mentor of sorts. I always loved animals and dogs, and when I turned ten years old, my parents got me a dog. Tinker was my responsibility—feeding, walking, and so on. I guess I did a good job because Tinker led to Woody—dog number two and Tinker's son.

My father and I walked our dogs together every morning on the nearby golf course before a sit-down breakfast. In the winter, we cross-country skied instead of walking. Those times were opportunities for him to mentor me, often by telling stories. One that stands out for me was the time he was eating breakfast at the Harvard Club in New York City and two fellows at the table next to his were deep in a discussion he couldn't avoid hearing. As soon as he realized they were executives from a major Stanley competitor and they were talking about important proprietary information, he got up and introduced himself. It never occurred to him to keep quiet and let them keep talking.

In his own life, my father was adamant about being balanced as a person. Nothing would get in the way of his exercise, his family time, and his career. He played squash during his lunch break at the New Britain YMCA, was home most nights for a sit-down family dinner and some TV with us kids, and was at his office by 8:30 a.m. every morning. In the winter, on Fridays he would drive a car full of kids to Vermont for ski weekends, returning on Sundays for another week of work.

He exercised despite his busy schedule, even when that busy schedule involved visiting me during my four years at Bowdoin College. An avid tennis player, my father refused to have his duties as a CEO and parent keep him from exercising and honing his game. So he had his new friend, the Bowdoin College tennis coach, set up a game of doubles with members of the men's tennis team whenever he was in town. Oddly, this little ritual led to him actually meeting my husband before I did, even though we were classmates. In fact, the details of their meeting were unknown to me until after I was married, when my husband, the former captain of the Bowdoin College tennis team, unwittingly revealed that throughout his four years he would get calls from the coach before certain event weekends at the college, instructing him that "Don Davis will be in town and to be at the courts by 9:00 a.m. Saturday" for a match. Who does that?

My father also loved sailing, and after he retired from Stanley, he competed weekly in summer boat races off Martha's Vineyard. These races involved sailing through a course marked off by buoys. Given the frequency in which these races took place, he was always having to find volunteers to crew his boat, whether it was his children or grandchildren. Crewing for him was always a learning experience for everyone involved. Often we were captained to take an unconventional tack, placing the vessel far away from the other racers, in arguably unchartered waters. Sometimes this experimentation with the wind and currents worked, leading to victory. Many times, however, it did not and often forfeited secure leads. But my father's approach to healthy competition was always the same. We participated not just to win but to challenge ourselves and to learn.

When I graduated from college, my father took me aside and said, "Ruthie, whatever you do in your life, you need to be honest and work hard. It may take you twice as long to get to the top, but you'll get there and stay there." He was proud of my career and was my mentor and confidant as I rose up the corporate ladder. I remember in my first corporate job—I was at Reebok—going to him with a dilemma. He told me, "Anything you do in the walls of your company, you should be fine with it being written on a billboard in the lobby of the building where everyone can see it." That nipped that situation in the bud.

I chose careers—the fashion industry and then an entrepreneurial venture—that were very different from my father's career, but his mantras have been equally applicable. I was really honored when he asked me to speak in his leadership class at MIT for duel degree graduate students focused on careers in manufacturing. I first spoke when I was a director at Reebok, then a VP at UGG and Tommy Hilfiger, and finally as the CEO of my own entrepreneurial start-up and eponymous shoe brand,

RUTHIE DAVIS. My father loved that I mixed things up a bit in his class. I was able to show how his mantras work in all kinds of businesses and in life.

The value I bring to the class and the reason they still like having me as a guest speaker is that as a fashion designer I've followed a different career path than many of the students. But at the end of the day, I *am* a manufacturer. I'm just manufacturing six-inch heels. I always bring a bag of shoes along with me when I speak in order to make the manufacturing connection.

The day I announced I was leaving my job as an executive with Tommy Hilfiger and starting my own company, my father was practical in saying that the odds were about one in a million that I would make it. He literally, in the beginning, was doubtful. After all, he was a corporate guy. That was his whole career, and that was where he was comfortable and what he understood. He wasn't the kind of father who would say no, but I had to go a little against his instincts. I give myself credit that I said, "Well, I'm doing this."

As time went on, he kept raising my odds. He went from "It's one in a million you're going to make it" to "OK, it's one in half a million." With time, he developed much more respect for me, that I was able to find my own path. It was the "I couldn't do it" type of respect. Before he died, he announced that he had raised my odds of success to "I think you're in the percentile that's going to make it." He told me I had achieved something he never did—I went after my own creative vision and dream. He was very proud of me. He learned from me that you can go after your dreams even if they seem a little pie in the sky. Dad was never afraid to keep learning, even if it was from the youngest of his six kids.

I remember when I was starting my own brand, I had a big conversation with him one day and said I thought he needed to add another mantra: "To be a good leader, you have to have passion." I wanted to add a creativity/passion mantra. I was always pushing, telling him, "You need this, Dad." It was key to how I had to lead my own company. I couldn't tell people to work hard. I could only inspire them to work hard by igniting their flame with my own energy, passion, and belief that anything's possible. In fact, he rewrote his mantras a number of times because they were an evolving thing, and, at one point, he included my passion mantra.

I challenged him in other ways too. On the days I talked to his class, he used to give me a lot of flak as we walked across the MIT campus because he thought I was dressed too high fashion. I was always wearing high-heel shoes that were too high and clothes that were too tight. One cold fall day, I had on this really cool aerodynamic jacket from Italy, black, sleek pants, and amazing shoes. "You look like a martian," he said. He wanted to tone me down. But my attitude was, how could I talk about my work and fashion-design vision without dressing that way? I think by the end of my talk, my ensemble made perfect sense to him.

My dad's journey was like that of any other human being. Obviously, nobody's perfect. He wasn't this god figure and didn't want to be. He liked people pushing him and wanted to learn. I think he got softer as he got older and more open minded. For example, one summer he let one of his grandsons, my nephew Luke, who studied botany at Penn State University, create a free-flowing, nontraditional garden at his home on Martha's Vineyard. He started to write children's books for his grandkids. And after much convincing, he agreed to forego his percolator for a streamlined Keurig.

His original attitude was, "Being the CEO is the best job in the company. If you can lead, do it. It's awesome." As he got older, he was forced to slow down and smell the roses. He became more open to different ways of getting to the end result. A person can be a leader in different ways, not only by running a huge company. I think that's an area where he grew.

I remember my father as a self-made man. He represented the best of what the United States has to offer. He was an old-school leader. He believed in ethics in business. He didn't succumb to fancy trappings and ego boosters. He was civically minded and involved in his community. He was a present father, husband, and friend, and most importantly, he treated the people who worked for him with respect, as equals and friends. He was the same guy in his personal life and in the work world.

My father was always talking about authenticity and integrity. He used to say to us kids, "There is one thing no one can ever take away from you—*only* you can give it away—and that's your integrity."

In his lifetime, he was a charismatic and übersuccessful leader, but what he was most proud of and what for him superseded his leadership was being a teacher. He felt his years teaching at MIT's Leaders for Global Operations (formerly Leaders for Manufacturing) program was his most important contribution. He was passionate about sharing his experiences and learnings with others. This was his life's greatest work and where he derived the most fulfillment and joy. Therefore, it was no surprise to me when my father chose that his tombstone would read "Leader and Teacher."

Preface

At his memorial service at MIT in 2012, our small group of former students celebrated Don Davis's love for life, teaching, and his family. We smiled when we remembered the precise way he would remove his glasses in class, connect his blue eyes with ours, and offer insight. We recalled his authenticity, how the man we knew as a teacher was the same person his children and his colleagues knew. We remembered that we consistently found him kind and approachable, that he made us comfortable in his presence, and that he had a sincere interest in each of us as an individual. Above all, we noted how often, in the most important leadership crucibles of our lives, we had all paused to ask, "What would Don do?"

Near the end of the service, Ruthie Davis spoke about her father. She revealed that he had begun work on a book about his leadership mantras, the maxims he had distilled from his own experiences and observations. Dan, Jon, and Stephen approached Jeff after the service and suggested that the best way to honor Don might be to complete his book.

The working title for Don's draft of the book was "Leaders Don't Choose Their Followers: Followers Choose Their Leaders." Don did not believe that merely by being appointed supervisor you were a leader; he believed you had to earn the support and commitment of a team to truly be a leader.

Don did not ask us to write this book, and he could not have expected we would write it. But would he have loved the idea? Absolutely. We were so moved both by the lessons he taught and by the man who took them to heart himself that we jumped at the chance to put his vision and wisdom into print. It was a way to make his vision our own.

Isn't the ability to gift one's vision and wisdom to other leaders the very definition of leadership?

Our fledgling book committee approached Ruthie, a regular guest speaker in Don's leadership class, to gauge her interest in supporting our efforts and joining the team. She enthusiastically agreed to participate. We met in June 2012 to begin an outline. We knew this was to be a leadership book. We knew we wanted to honor Don Davis. We considered a straightforward explanation of his mantras and how they might be applied by leaders. But, in discussing Don's mantras, we and other alumni kept returning to our own stories. We decided to change course and began to gather a collection of significant, personal anecdotes from Don's students supporting the leadership mantras he taught us.

We next approached Bill Hanson, who had taken over teaching the Leaders for Global Operations (LGO) leadership seminar when Don retired. Bill's work with Don gave him a unique perspective on Don's impact. He shared with us some quotes he had collected from Don's former students:

> "He didn't talk about equations; he talked about integrity and the reality of balancing your life. He talked about conviction."
> "Don revealed himself in a very authentic way and in doing so, people trusted him and followed him."
> "In the end, he seemed to be telling us, leadership is emotional and very hard. You can't lead without taking some risk that you will care too much."

Bill was enthusiastic about our project, and he pushed us to frame the book not around memories of Don but around Don's wisdom for today's and tomorrow's leaders.

Collecting leadership stories reflecting what we had learned from Don excited us, and we believed the approach novel. We were optimistic that we'd finish the book in six months. As we attempted to turn passionate memories into engaging narratives, we discovered we were wildly optimistic. These stories took time to write, and all of our storytellers had full-time jobs.

We sought help. Through Bob Thomas, a former MIT professor and currently the executive director of the Accenture Institute for High Performance, we were introduced to Kent Lineback and Carol Franco, an exceptional writing/editing team with a long track record of success in the leadership genre. Their skilled interviewing and editing drew out the authenticity in each storyteller, bringing Don's mantras to life.

We know Don would want this book to provoke thoughtful discussion of real-life situations. We know he would want it to both teach and inspire, for the two are inextricably linked. So, we've produced a guidebook about leadership.

This book is intended for practicing or aspiring leaders. It is full of the lessons Don taught, reflected in the experiences and words of his students as they went out into the world and faced the risky, grueling dilemmas of leadership. As Don liked to remind every leader who would listen, "Good leadership doesn't just make a difference, it makes all the difference."

Stephen, Ruthie, Dan, Jon, and Jeff

Introduction

You get your first big plant management job running a giant factory that makes pickups. You pour your heart and soul into your work. Six months in, the economy crashes and the company decides to close the plant in six months. You've come to care deeply about the hundreds of people who work there. You know the closure will mark the end of a life many of them won't be able to re-create. How do you tell them what's going to happen? How do you lead them to continue producing quality product to the very end? *What would you do?*

A large customer owes your business $10 million. Wall Street is judging your performance based on quarterly cash flow, which also affects executive bonuses, and so you have a strong incentive to collect the money before quarter end. You convince your customer to pay, and they bring you the check just after midnight at quarter end. Your boss calls the next day to ask if you've received the money. When you say you have, he asks, "When did you get the check in your hand?" *What would you do?*

You take over a large division of a medical-device company. The board of directors is watching your performance closely. You want to do well because you hope to be a candidate when a higher-level position opens up in a year or less. Your team's most important target is revenue growth. Late in the year, you discover that your top sales executives are grossly abusing the company's expense policy, maliciously undermining the agreed-upon business direction at every turn, and pressuring members of the sales team to keep quiet. You decide to fire them outright, but then you realize the short-term turmoil that creates will probably make you miss your sales targets for the current year and part of the next. *What would you do?*

These dilemmas come directly from the twenty-one stories that make up the bulk of this book. Each is told by an actual leader describing a leadership crisis he or she had to resolve. Each contains sufficient information to understand the problem, what the narrator chose to do, and the consequences. Every storyteller is a graduate of MIT's Leaders for Global Operations (LGO) program, where Don taught leadership for over twenty years. Storytellers include men and women in positions that range from first-line supervisor to plant manager, entrepreneur, business unit head, CEO, and nonprofit leader.

In spite of this diversity, you will find in their situations, struggles, emotions, and decisions much that rings true to your own experiences. It will be easy for you to put yourself in their shoes. What won't be easy is answering the question posed above: *What would you do?*

Leadership is more often about painful, difficult choices than it is about moments of glory, because a leader must frequently put private success and career at risk. Hence, the stories are deeply personal. In each, the storyteller must step back and ask, "Who am I as a leader? What do I consider most important and valuable?"

Not every story is about success. Some show failure and the difficult learning that can come from it. Some stories are disguised, not to shield the storyteller but most often for reasons of confidentiality that will be obvious in the details of the stories themselves. Nonetheless, disguised or not, each is based on actual events.

We appreciate the willingness of these leaders to tell their stories. We suspect one reason they felt comfortable revealing their human and imperfect experiences was an inspiring teacher they all shared: Don Davis.

Don honed his deep understanding of leadership over a long, productive career that began as a naval officer during World War II. After the war and an MBA from Harvard Business School, he joined the

Stanley Works in 1948, where he became executive vice president in 1962 and CEO in 1966.

Don saw the explosive growth opportunity the do-it-yourself market would create for tools and hardware, and he pushed Stanley to develop the products consumers would need to build things themselves, growing the company from $230 million in 1966 to $2 billion when he retired. When big-box retailing took off in the early 1980s, Stanley was perfectly positioned, and the name remains a strong brand with consumers to this day.

Don's corporate and community leadership extended well beyond The Stanley Works. He served as the chairman of the National Association of Manufacturers, the Connecticut Business and Industry Association (as a founder), and the National Institute for Dispute Resolution. At various times, he was also a director of public companies including AlliedSignal Corporation, Pitney Bowes, Connecticut Mutual Life Insurance Company, and Dexter Manufacturing Company. Don's leadership extended to many aspects of the community where he and most of the Stanley employees lived. He served on the New Britain General Hospital board and the local New Britain YMCA board (where he also played squash every day). He donated the Don Davis Tennis Courts in Walnut Hill Park in New Britain.

In 1990, after retiring from Stanley, Don boldly walked into the offices of MIT's nascent Leaders for Manufacturing (now LGO) program. Having heard good things about the program's mission to increase the competitiveness of US manufacturing companies, he offered to help complete the curriculum with a seminar focused on leadership and ethics. For compensation he requested only a parking pass and access to the tennis and squash courts.

Founded in 1988, the mission of the LGO program was to create a new source of leadership talent that combined management expertise and technical depth. Program graduates all receive an MS in an engineering discipline and an MBA from the Sloan School in two years. Each class of roughly fifty students shares experiences ranging from an intense first summer of required classwork to myriad plant tours, a six-month internship at one of the program's several dozen industrial partners, and the very popular elective course, Leadership and Ethics, that Don established and taught for over twenty years.

Don's six hundred students are part of an alumni body that now numbers more than one thousand LGO graduates. Though the program's roots began with "saving American manufacturing," its reach quickly extended to companies and operations across the world.

Why would Don take on this challenge? He had headed a US manufacturing company for two decades, of course, but the real reason was something he explained later. When he was a sophomore at Penn State, someone had taken the time to tell him that he had the skills to be a good leader and that "Good leadership doesn't just make a difference, it makes all the difference." Don called this his wake-up call, and it started him on his journey to be the best leader he could be and to deliver a similar wake-up call to others.

Don built his MIT class around a fairly simple approach, the same approach we take in this book. He shared his leadership principles—he called them his leadership mantras—and illustrated them through his own leadership stories and those of prominent guests from business, politics, sports, and entertainment (nearly always close friends), who shared the intimate details of their own experiences with each class.

Don continually refined and added to his mantras—he saw them as fluid. He didn't require students to memorize them or treat them as laws. They simply served as guideposts for the rich discussions he led and for all his students as they made their way forward as leaders themselves. (A full list of his mantras follows this introduction.)

Each story in this book includes key moments where the leader has to make a tough decision. A guiding principle Don often used, "Do the right thing," captures the quintessence of his mantras—mantras like "Integrity is the bedrock of effective leadership; only you can lose your integrity" or "Followers choose leaders they trust, respect, and are comfortable with." Many of the mantras do more than suggest appropriate actions and decisions; they supply the backbone for moments when leaders may be tempted to choose the easy way out.

Don also knew his students were at the beginning of their careers and likely to be given authority soon after they graduated. And so, in another mantra, he reminded them that "Leaders need a base of power and authority, but the more a leader uses this power, the less there is left." Like Don, who became CEO of The Stanley Works in his early forties, most of our storytellers were among the youngest people at their hierarchical level. Without Don, they may not have thought much about how quickly positional power could be used up or about other, better ways to exercise influence.

Don also knew from experience that "The number of effective leadership styles is limitless." He encouraged each student to "Be yourself," because he knew that authenticity displayed consistently and over time could build significant leadership power. Consequently, you will see in these stories copious self-reflection and learning among the storytellers as we watch them pass through significant inflection points on their personal journeys.

Though none of Don's mantras says explicitly "Do the right thing," this notion permeates all of them. In 2002, during a time of corporate ethics scandals, Don delivered a speech to the LGO alums. As he did with his most impassioned talks in class, he punctuated key sections with a pause, a deep stare with his piercing blue eyes, and a practiced flick of his oft-removed reading glasses. He said:

> So, as companies try to reinvent themselves for the future—what principles from the past do you as a leader need to hold onto?
>
> Build trust in all directions with all your constituents and all your stakeholders. Trust cannot be legislated—you have to earn it. And you do this by being a leader of unquestioned integrity—an authentic human being who has a highly developed sense of straightness and fairness in all human interactions. As a leader, your ethical standards will have a major impact based on your behavior, not your words...
>
> It takes courage and a sense of self-worth, together with a certain amount of wisdom, to stay off that slippery slope of temptation. But, when you do the right thing (and you'll know what it is), you win in every direction—and at every level of the organization.

Those of us who knew Don get chills every time we read this passage, because the leadership that really makes a difference is the kind that returns a beaming smile upon self-reflection. Leadership can be exhausting, but it also feels damn good.

We solicited these real-world stories from Don's former students. We told LGO alums that we wanted them to share the most gut-wrenching decisions of their careers for the benefit of others. Though some stories are disguised, we don't believe this detracts from their value as leadership learning tools.

Let us be clear. Though these stories were occasioned by Don and they reflect his leadership lessons, they are not *about* Don Davis. This is a book about leadership, an attempt to preserve the most timeless of Don's teachings for future generations of leaders.

Don grew up in a different age. He preferred longhand letters to e-mail and retired from executive management before the World Wide Web was born. Yet his insights remain timeless—especially regarding how to motivate human teams to achieve performance well beyond reasonable expectations.

We offer these stories as occasions for self-reflection and learning as you work on improving your performance during the leadership moments of your work and life. Read them, put yourself in the shoes of the men and women who experienced and wrote them, and ask yourself, *What would I do?* Compare your responses to the thoughts and behaviors of our storytellers. We strongly suspect that such reflection will help you become a better leader and you too may begin to ask, "What would Don do?"

Don Davis Leadership Mantras

- Leaders don't choose their followers. Followers choose their leaders.
- Followers choose leaders they trust, respect, and are comfortable with.
- Integrity is the bedrock of effective leadership. Only you can lose your integrity.
- Selfship is the enemy of leadership.
- Leadership should be viewed as stewardship.
- Leaders need a base of power and authority. But the more a leader uses this power, the less there is left.
- Be yourself. The number of effective leadership styles is limitless.
- The best leadership is based on persuasion.
- Leaders set the ethical standards and tone of the organization by their behavior.
- One of a leader's key responsibilities is stamping out self-serving politics when it emerges.
- Be sure to know as much as possible about the people you are leading.
- One manages things; people lead people.
- Diversity in an organization is not only legally required and socially desirable, but it is effective.
- Don't make tough, borderline decisions until you need to. Many will solve themselves with time.
- Be quick to praise, but slow to admonish. Praise in public, but admonish in private.
- When making decisions about people, listen to your gut.

- Almost everyone can see through manipulation and game playing. Everyone can spot a phony.
- Learn to say out loud, "I was wrong" and "I don't know."
- If you know a plan or decision is wrong, don't implement it. Instead, keep talking.
- Each of us has the potential to lead, follow, or be an individual contributor.

CHAPTER 1

Don't Let a Leadership Opportunity Go By

Charlie Hix

I t's nighttime in Everett, Washington, and it's pouring rain. I'm standing outside the Boeing factory, its doors wide open with all the lights on, and I'm staring at a long line of 777 jetliners, one behind the other, in various stages of completion. It's my second evening on the job. I felt like a conductor standing on the track, holding back the train just so we could finish that last little thing. I thought the weight of the whole factory was resting on my shoulders.

My job was to manage the crew that finished each airplane before it rolled out of the factory. We had the last six days of work on the triple seven production line. From there the airplane moved to the flight line, where it was painted, fueled, flight-tested, and finally delivered to the customer. It was an important area. Anything that didn't get done right—any missing parts or remaining issues—needed to get fixed at the factory door.

As we prepared our airplane for rollout that night, we discovered a leak in the pneumatic system that provided high-pressure air from the engines into the air-conditioning system. The leak could be anywhere. Taking the airplane apart to fix it was something we preferred not to do once it had rolled out and been painted.

This was my first rollout. It typically occurred around ten o'clock at night. The rollout opened up space to "move the line" so every airplane behind it could move forward on the assembly line. In those days moving the line took about five hours of unproductive time, so it was important that it went off like clockwork.

We were within an hour of rollout, and we hadn't fixed the leak. I was beginning to wonder what would happen if we didn't find it in time. As they started hooking the tug to the airplane, folks in charge of the factory were warning me that bad things were going to happen to me if I jeopardized moving the line.

When I had been introduced to my area and crew a day or so earlier, the crew members had let me know that in the last eighteen months, they'd had nine different managers. One of the crusty old guys said, "Yeah, and I give you about a month or two." As I stood outside in the dark and the rain, I was afraid it might be more like a day or two.

This was a new experience for me. I'd worked in engineering for Boeing for eight years. But I'd never been a manager prior to attending LGO. Actually, Boeing had sponsored me to go back to MIT. I always felt fortunate to have had that experience. It was like getting struck by lightning, but in a good way. Sometimes I asked myself how this kid from a mountain town in Colorado, a product of a little public school, managed to be there with some of those industry leaders, taking a leadership class with Don Davis, who had run The Stanley Works for twenty years as the CEO.

When I returned to Boeing after graduation, I became a first-line manager for a team of about twenty-five union-represented mechanics, many of whom were older than I was, had more experience, and had been building airplanes for many years. Here I was, a brand-new manager, new to the area, right there at the factory door, leading that team. I was feeling the pressure.

I had begun my career in propulsion engineering, where we looked after the engines and fuel system and anything associated with them. As an engineer I sat at my desk doing analysis work. So, while I knew a lot about the airplane and how it operated technically, I knew very little about the actual build process of the airplane. The factory was a big, black box, a foreign environment.

It has improved over the years, but back then there was little interaction in the company between engineers and the folks who actually built the airplanes. I had experienced at least one strike by factory workers and recalled driving through one of the gates while the strike was underway. Engineers were required to be at our desks, but the burning barrels and picket signs we drove through were reminders of the tension.

The engineering and factory work environments are as different as the stereotypes would lead you to expect. Engineers are often shy, even awkward, and speak in hushed tones while working in front of their computers in button-down shirts and pocket protectors. Meanwhile, factory workers wear coveralls over their jeans, T-shirts, and tattoos and show up for work before dawn on their Harley-Davidson motorcycles, rain or shine. They have to shout at one another in order to be heard over the din of rivet guns and heavy machinery.

I was assigned to second shift. Most of the management and support personnel were available during a normal day shift—morning to afternoon or early evening. Then the second shift took over around 4:00 p.m. and worked until eleven o'clock or midnight, when a skeleton crew on third shift worked through the night doing maintenance, moving equipment, or performing tasks with some risk associated. Second shift was the place they put people who had enough experience to know how to get things done and didn't need a lot of support. Someone told me before I accepted the job, "Well, that might be a good thing to do after you've been a manager in some other area that's a little more white collar. Don't change too many things at once."

But I recalled some of the things Don had said, especially "Don't let a leadership opportunity go by." That was the reason I agreed to second shift. I could have said, "You ought to leave me on day shift" or "Look for something closer to my comfort zone." But when second shift was suggested, I said, "Well, yeah, sure, let's try it."

Don often spoke to us about pushing ourselves outside our comfort zones and looking at challenges that came along and just saying yes. Jump into the deep water, if you will. I had Don's teachings fresh under my belt—how to work with people, how to lead. I also had business experience as well as a technical career behind me. So I thought, *This is a golden opportunity to learn.* Still, personally, it seemed very high risk.

While the basic structure of the airplane was complete when we got it, we still had six days of work to do before it was ready for rollout. We installed engines and other expensive parts. We jacked it and swung the landing gear to make sure it extended and retracted normally. We "woke up" the plane by applying power and testing all the systems—hydraulic, pneumatic, electrical—that could be tested indoors. We "got the blood flowing" around the airplane and made sure everything worked.

With over one hundred thousand parts, much could go wrong. Inevitably, there were items that needed to be fixed or replaced. So we had to do any troubleshooting that needed to be done, and, at the same time, we had to keep the production line moving. Because we were getting right down to a committed delivery date, the pressures were extremely high to ensure that we made our commitment to the customer with a quality airplane that was perfect.

As I waited on that dark, rainy night, my first rollout, with the factory manager breathing down my neck, the crew finally isolated the leak. It was in a section between the wing and fuselage (the body of the plane)—a very tough area to reach. One of the crew was tucked up in there so far I could only see his feet.

"Got it!" he suddenly shouted. "Pull me out!"

We reconnected the high-pressure air supply. Success! The system held pressure. I was elated, and so was the crew. We'd just made the deadline for rollout. Maybe I would last a month or two.

But a minute later, I heard another one of my guys shout out an expletive in frustration. "FOD in the pack inlet—tough to get—long way in!" he called out.

What he saw was a piece of foreign object debris. A plastic cap had fallen deep into the inlet of the air-conditioning heat exchanger. We needed to fish that cap out before it caused any problems.

Now I really was holding up the line. The deadline had come and gone, and my plane was still sitting there.

Even my crew members, who were very seasoned, were telling me, "Let it go. They'll catch it downstream. Just write a tag," which was the paper work for moving problems down the line. "Don't worry about it," they said. "Don't get yourself in trouble. Just let it go." But I thought, *You know, it's the right thing to do to finish this, even if it jeopardizes being exactly on schedule. Let's not pass it downstream. It will be a bigger problem for someone else later on.*

"Just give us five more minutes," I kept saying to the guy in charge, who was one step away from calling my boss. And I proceeded to "five more minutes" him for close to an hour. I was sweating bullets.

Finally, we managed to pull that plastic cap from its deep hiding place, and when they started to pull the airplane out of the factory, the crew erupted with high fives and pure elation for completing what we needed to do. Their reputation depended on that. If they sent problems downstream, the guys there would talk and poke back at them. I realized that I had given my crew the opportunity to feel good about that airplane. It also showed them I was willing to stick my neck out and do the right thing, not just take the easy way out.

After the airplane left and our shift was over, I looked around at the crew. The last time I remembered feeling like that was when I was on a high school football team that had won a really tough game. The entire crew of twenty-five had pitched in to do whatever needed to be done—running and fetching things, checking something out, getting the airplane ready to move—knowing that part of the crew was tied up on trying to finish the job. People put in the extra effort.

It made me think more about Don in terms of doing the right thing, even if there are personal risks. I give Don credit for my jumping into the deep end and taking that first job right out of school. I also credit Don with making sure that, even when times get tough, when you're the leader, you need to do the right thing. Plus, you have to model the right behavior. Don would talk about that too. So there were a lot of times, as I think back, where Don would make his ideas—his mantras—come alive. He would state the mantra, tell a story that reinforced it, and explain how he learned it.

I stayed with that crew for over a year, probably three months longer than my boss wanted me to. But I wanted to make a statement that it's not right for a team to constantly experience a fluid situation with leadership. I left that crew in a much better position than I found it. Its productivity and quality were better. Those people saw someone who was willing to stand up for them, do the right thing, and wasn't just there for eight hours to do whatever it took to marginally get the job done. I treated them with respect, which, in those environments, hadn't always been the case. When I left that team, not only had we bonded together, they had bonded better with each other. I felt very positive about that experience.

Doing the right thing so early in my management role was formative because I was in a risky environment. But Don and others had taught me to trust my instincts. Treat people with respect, and, while it might take a while, they'll respond. Set a positive expectation of someone, and you'll build a relationship. Once that relationship is built, they won't want to let you down. Whether it was Don's mantras or other things that I walked in the door with, here was an opportunity to try them out. What I discovered was that if I stuck with them for a while, they really worked.

To this day, and it may sound corny, I still get emotional when I think about that rainy night in Everett. As we rolled that airplane out, one of the mechanics came over to me—someone I'd known for just a couple of days—and he high-fived me because he was so happy we had completed that work. I thought, *Wow! I didn't realize that my stopping the process and saying, "No, let's finish this" would ever cause anybody to do that.* Here I was, a manager, expecting to be treated like an adversary. Yet this guy came right up to me and gave me a high five. He was so excited about what we had done. I still have that stupid plastic cap.

CHAPTER 2

Leadership Is All about the Long Run

Anonymous

The call came at noon while my family and I were at my sister's wedding in Santa Fe. There had been an accident at one of the chemical plants in the business I managed. The plant manager didn't have many details yet. He just knew that one worker, John, was in critical condition with third-degree burns over most of his body.

Trained as a chemical engineer, I had worked in complicated chemical plants long enough to know what questions to ask. Was everyone else safe? Was the fire extinguished? Was there any leakage or environmental impact on the river below? And, above all, was John at the best medical center in the area, and did his family know? The manager promised to keep me posted.

I returned to my family, numb with grief and already wondering about the root cause.

The identity of the storyteller, as well as those of companies, other people, and locations in the story, has been disguised. Any similarity to actual people or companies is coincidental.

Though John had performed this procedure hundreds of times, was there something wrong with our training? Did our maintenance procedures lead to a mechanical failure?

As soon as we could, my wife and I packed up our infants and flew back to Delaware. I dropped them off and took a flight to the plant in Kentucky. John passed away at 3:00 a.m. that night.

The business I ran was part of Diversified Companies (DC), where it was something of an anomaly. Next to DC's high-tech aerospace and pharmaceutical businesses, we produced basic organic chemicals in three plants, including the one in Kentucky. Ours was the oldest business in the company. In spite of its age, it was a good, steady business staffed with highly competent people.

It was also a business where DC put rising management stars, an ideal first job with profit-and-loss responsibility. Starting with DC in operations, I'd changed positions every two years or so, adding large chunks of responsibility with each move. Now, at thirty, I was running my own business. I relished the chance to learn and own every aspect: sales, marketing, finance, technology, and operations. I was sure we'd make our quarterly targets and that my operations background would contribute meaningfully to safety, quality, and cost performance. I was impatient to learn and move ahead.

I flew to Kentucky to represent the company at John's funeral and to offer my condolences to John's wife and children. I stayed the rest of the week, working with plant and corporate teams, plus OSHA and state authorities, to understand what happened. I had to decide what to do next, and for that I needed to immerse myself and make my own observations.

John's job that evening had been to transfer a chemical product from one large holding tank to another in the tank farm at the plant. The farm was a vast collection of tanks, connected by pipes and valves, much like you see around an oil refinery. To do the job, a routine task he had done hundreds of times, John needed to clean a transfer pipe with steam and then open valves to route the chemical from one tank to another through the pipe. It appeared that John had not opened the relief valve, so the high-pressure steam simply built up in the pipe. Then, when John opened the valve to release the chemical—which was heated so it could flow through the pipe—from the source tank, condensate from the pipe shot back into the hot tank, blew off the top, and rained molten chemical down on him and set him on fire. A big, burly, ex-high school football star, John made it several hundred yards back to the control room, where his teammates—all trained in first aid—covered and rolled him to put out the flames and called for an ambulance.

At his funeral in this small Kentucky town, a company town, the line to get to the viewing was five blocks long. The whole town was standing in line. I was obviously the corporate guy there. I'll never forget it. It was the hardest thing I've ever done.

On the plane ride home, I tried to come to terms with what happened and what to do about it. The manual valves in the tank farm that John had operated were standard in the industry at that time. Automatic, computer-controlled valves are standard now, but they were just beginning to appear then. Installing them would have required a huge investment and significant operational disruption. However, with their installation, what happened to John would likely never happen again.

Though the company was formally absolved of responsibility for the accident, I just didn't feel right. I knew that we could continue to operate the business, generate plenty of cash, and that I would move to a larger general management position relatively soon. But was this really the right thing to do? I kept asking myself what Don Davis would have done.

Not only had Don been a memorable teacher at MIT, he was directly involved in me going to work for DC. As I had been finishing LGO and interviewing with various prospective employers, none of which felt right, I'd found myself washing my hands in a restroom next to Don. "You found a job you want?" he'd said.

"No."

"What are you looking for?" I'd told him, and he'd said, "You'll get a call tomorrow."

The next day I got a call from Jerry Mountz, the president of DC. A gruff New Yorker, he said, "Hey, Don tells me you're a great kid and you're looking for the right company. This could be a perfect match for you."

I flew to Delaware the next day and interviewed with the top management team. At the end of the day, they offered me a staff job in finance at headquarters. I turned it down. "Thank you," I said. "I'm grateful, but I want to get my hands dirty. I'm probably going to spend most of my life in corporate jobs and I want to have credibility when I talk about what happens in operations." The next day they offered me a job at a struggling plastics plant in Georgia.

From there, I was on the fast track, moving ahead every couple of years. When I began agitating to run a business, DC put me in charge of the $200 million organic chemicals business with the three plants. I felt that I was on track to run really big, complicated, important businesses.

On the plane home from Kentucky, I thought about the company and the business I was running. Ours was a highly progressive and lauded company, known for consistent performance at scale. The company had several businesses on the cutting edge of technology and was investing heavily in them, and then it had my business, which had long passed its heyday and was in fact a cash cow. It was meeting current standards for environmental impact and safety, but it didn't seem to belong in this company I was so proud of. My mind raced through ways to eliminate the possibility of a recurrence of the events of that week.

The problem was that the economics didn't work. Left alone and well managed, without much investment, it was a good business. But the investment required to upgrade the control systems would be enormous because we would have to rebuild most of the operations. We couldn't justify it, given the stock market's expectations of financial return.

Yet, if we kept the business and didn't invest in it, I felt we weren't being true to the company's vision. We were allowing mediocrity to creep into a portfolio that was mostly superb. Without automatic controls there was some likelihood of human error, and someone years down the road was going to get the same kind of call that I'd gotten. I didn't think that was OK.

By the end of my flight home, I knew the right thing to do: close down at least part of the business to simplify the operation and sell it to another company for which it would be strategically important. As I made up my mind, I thought of Don. It was, very simply, "What would Don do?" and the answer was, "Do the right thing," and the right thing was to get the business in the hands of someone for whom the right investments would make sense.

When I returned I confirmed that the company was unlikely to make a major investment in an upgrade of operations. But when I talked about selling the business, some in the company wondered what I was thinking. "Yes, it was a tragedy," they said, "but do we really need to sell something that generates such a nice return? Besides, no one will buy it. Don't mess with it."

Many of my peers said I was wasting my time. The company would make more money by just continuing to operate the thing. "Why would you want to rock the boat?" they said. "This was terrible for John and his family. You're sad. But what you need to do is just ride it out, continue to improve the business, and keep doing the great job you were doing before this happened. Then, get out and move on to your next thing."

When I persisted, I could sense some colleagues and others distancing themselves from me. I wasn't naive. I understood there was real risk of damaging the reputation I'd built. I didn't know how long it would take to find a buyer, do the deal, get permission from all the government agencies involved, and wrap it up. I had no idea how this whole effort would turn out.

Senior management could not understand at first what I was doing. I was worried they would question my business judgment and that my star would fall. At that age I believed that several lost years in my career could mean the difference between long-term success and failure.

Still, it didn't feel right. Someone had to worry about the long-term consequences of doing nothing. Eventually I was able to convince the company to let me, as a hobby, play around with trying to find a buyer. I'm sure they all thought there was little chance I could get a deal done, in part because the environmental issues were complicated, given the age and nature of the business.

I committed to completing a deal because I knew if I stopped halfway, if I found a buyer and got it started and then moved on, that there was a very high likelihood the process would stop. It would go back to the status quo, which was comfortable for everybody.

I set aside my own qualms about reputation and career, ignored everyone who wondered what I was doing, and went to work finding a buyer.

There weren't many options. In the end, I had one real chance. At a trade show, I met with the president of a company whose business focused on the products that were a sideline and anachronism for DC. We agreed to continue the conversation over the coming weeks.

It turned out this company wanted to buy key parts of our business and offered enough money that we could shut down part of our operation, reduce our exposure, simplify what we did, and make it safer. That makes it sound simple, but it wasn't. As I began negotiating with the president of this company, I updated DC's finance and legal teams and my boss. No one was optimistic. The deal had a small chance of happening, we probably wouldn't be paid enough, and our quarterly results would take a big hit.

Though long-term safety of our workforce drove me, I couldn't help but worry that so many of them would lose their jobs. I had worked on a plant closure once before. That experience taught me to make the business decision rationally, but to spend every moment after the decision was approved worrying about the people who would be impacted. I knew with severance and other kinds of support that we would take care of these people. If we got this deal approved, I would travel to the plant to convey the news myself.

Meanwhile, I was saying no to requests to consider other jobs, and I worked harder on the deal. I knew there must be an arrangement that would satisfy most of our company's short-term objectives, prove acceptable to the buyer, and reduce our company's long-term risk. After months of work with the prospective buyer, we reached an agreement. I pitched our senior management—several times, in fact—and they finally agreed to the deal, except for one last step.

David Lines, a DC executive who worked for the CEO and someone I knew and respected immensely, wanted to confirm that I had done the right thing. He took me with him on one of the company jets to sit down with the president of the buyer, have dinner, and talk through the deal and why the buyer wanted to do it. On the plane there and back, David drilled into every aspect of the deal with me, checking my judgment. Satisfied, he supported the deal, and we went ahead.

I thought it was done, but it wasn't because at this point the government weighed in, only now it was the Justice Department rather than the environmental regulators. Government lawyers wanted to review the transaction. Because there were few firms left in the industry, the deal might concentrate too much economic power in one firm. After a short initial review, the government sent us a second request, which I learned might take months to resolve.

This was hard for me to take. I had worked on this deal for six months, and I thought it was finished, only to find out the government was saying, "We're not sure we're going to let this happen." Even if they finally approved the deal, responding to their request would take more months. After all our work, there was a chance the sale might not happen at all. I was tired and frustrated. The perfect next job was waiting, and it might not wait long enough for me to complete the transaction. What would Don Davis do? That turned out to be easy to answer: finish the process. It was the right thing to do, and that's what I did.

We prepared with our lawyers for the trip to Washington, DC, months later. The deposition was grueling. Shortly after that, the government approved the transaction. I did move on to another job. Several large parts of the plant were shut down. Some workers moved on, but the ones who stayed were safer.

CHAPTER *3*

Find the Balance between Short and Long Run

Anonymous

"I was chairman at Stanley Works for eighty quarters."

I'll always remember the first time I heard Don say that. He said it quite a bit that semester, if memory serves, but the first time you hear a quote like that is always the most memorable. At the time I was a spry twenty-five years of age, and although I found the quote to be as amusing then as I do today in my early forties, my understanding of Don's true meaning in saying it—or perhaps, better put, my interpretation of Don's meaning in saying it—has evolved considerably over the years.

At that time and at my age then, my measures of time were different. Having only spent three years in the "real" world between undergrad and grad school, I was still living in a world where semesters were the most meaningful measure of time. Given that I equated one semester with one

---

The identity of the storyteller, as well as those of companies, other people, and locations in the story, has been disguised. Any similarity to actual people or companies is coincidental.

fiscal quarter, eighty quarters roughly translated to "eternity"…plus or minus a semester. What did Don mean then when he said he was chairman at Stanley for eighty quarters? Clearly it meant that he felt like he was there for an eternity, or so I thought over fifteen years ago.

As my experience back in the real world grew to dozens of quarters, Don's veiled meaning definitely shifted. Through several roles at a couple of companies over a decade, I concluded that the mindset and decision-making paradigm that focused on current quarter results to the near exclusion of all else was both dangerous and all too prevalent in corporate America. In the best cases, future implications or consequences simply received no consideration. Only the current quarter mattered. In the worst cases, decision-makers knew they were deliberately mortgaging future results to optimize those of the present. "We have ninety days to figure out how we'll dig out of the hole this will create next quarter." Was *this*—don't focus on the present and ignore the future—what Don had meant? If it was, and I definitely thought it was at the time, he was right, and I absolutely got it. What a struggle it must have been, I thought, to constantly battle that way of thinking for twenty years, from the chairman's seat or any other. Don was preparing us for that very battle.

As time passed and my responsibilities grew, my issues with this way of thinking and operating continued to grow as well. I was never one to shy away from pushing back on direction I felt was flawed—another key message Don always underscored, having the courage of your convictions. But the level at which I found myself pushing back was becoming more and more daunting, even for someone as seemingly confident as I. "If I were the founder," I would proclaim, "and this were 'My Company Inc.,' we would not be doing things this way. We would focus almost exclusively on initiatives, decisions, and actions that result in the best value creation for our shareholders and experiences for our customers in the longest possible terms." (Or something like that.)

Of course, such rhetoric increasingly elicited responses like, "Great! Then why don't you go start My Company Inc. and do just that?" from an ever-more impressive cast of leaders.

Fast-forward a few more years, and I was doing just that. The company was not My Company Inc., but it was a publicly traded technology design and manufacture company, and I was named its president and CEO.

To say that we focused on creating value and customer relationships for the long term would be a great understatement. Every member of the new senior team I brought in shared my distaste for the overly tactical, quarter-to-quarter focus that we had all seen in our careers to date and was eager to start running a business in a different way. For example, we replaced the ninety-day sales focus of the previous leadership with a more comprehensive five-year opportunity pipeline. The short-term research-and-development "science experiments" (as we sarcastically called them) were replaced with a rolling three-year technology road map. The month-to-month leasing of disparate facilities stretching halfway across the globe was replaced by an eight-year facilities consolidation and asset optimization plan. There were countless other examples as well, which meant we, finally, were running a business the way we always thought one should be run. At least we were running it that way right up to the point after nine months when we went bankrupt.

Actually, the bankruptcy was planned—a necessary step for the future that we took with our eyes clearly focused on the horizon. Unfortunately, the bankruptcy didn't go as we had hoped.

It had been clear when my team and I took over that the company was in trouble. It was burning through cash for many reasons—above all, because we had to pay for the extensive manufacturing facilities the previous management had built in anticipation of rapidly growing sales, which had not materialized. Our solution was to revenue our way out of the problem. By concentrating on channel development, we were quickly able to grow our sales pipeline fivefold—enough to soak up and pay for our unused manufacturing capacity.

The problem was the long sales cycle in our industry, which was new to us. Getting from a sale to full production required a test or pilot phase of twelve to eighteen months, followed by a ramp-up phase of another twelve to eighteen months—in total, two to three years from deal to full revenue. That was obviously not going to work. We had a long-term, strategic solution and a tactical, short-term problem.

In addition, we were bleeding from a thousand cash cuts. Previous management had condoned and even encouraged a culture of experimentation without any accounting or engineering process controls. Company engineers had committed to dozens of start-up projects with outsiders, funded by the company, which no one outside engineering knew about. The way we began to discover this problem was our inability to forecast accounts payable. Every week, every month, we seemed to owe considerably more than anyone had anticipated. The reason, we finally worked out, was that no one outside the engineering group knew about any of these projects until the bills started to arrive.

All this became clear about halfway into my nine-month tenure, and we realized then that we needed to go Chapter 11 and restructure. Our plan was to sell manufacturing assets and become a technology company that focused on design and outsourced manufacturing.

It was a great plan that, we believed, would work, but a majority on the board couldn't bring themselves to go along. Two reasons prevailed. Some members couldn't stomach sending jobs overseas, even nonexistent jobs that were unlikely ever to exist anywhere, given our current flight path headed straight for the ground. Other members came from a manufacturing mentality that said real men had factories and built what they sold. Whatever their reasons, we ran out of time to change their minds. And when they refused to part with the company's manufacturing capabilities, my team and I resigned. The company still exists and, ironically, it seems to be slowly implementing the asset-shedding strategy we espoused—but so slowly and halfheartedly that there's a good chance Chapter 11 will become Chapter 7, complete shutdown.

After a career of consistent success prior to that point, I had to face failure as the CEO and leader of this firm. Don said we would experience failure and we should learn from it. First lesson: before that experience, I had been convinced of my own ability; I believed there was nothing I couldn't fix. Now, I learned that isn't true. I'm as flawed as any other senior leader out there. I know now I can't fix everything. There are things you can fix and things you can't fix. You need to learn how to recognize up front what's unfixable.

There were more lessons. If I had looked more carefully at the industry I was entering as a CEO, I might not have even taken the job. I rightly believed this company had superior technology and the future of the industry was bright, but success required more than that. It required dealing right away with the messy short-term problems, including the cash leakage and, not least, the board. We should have raised the possibility of Chapter 11 right away. With more time, we might have convinced the board of its necessity.

Above all, I have had to appreciate the personal irony of going bankrupt in my first real opportunity to set the long-term direction of a business and rein in some of the actions and decisions that optimized the short-term at the expense of the future.

So, other than the countless things, short term and long, that we could and should have done more, better, or differently—or not done at all—what was the fundamental insight here? What would Don say about what happened? He made it eighty quarters! Why did I barely make three?

The answer, I ultimately found, came in tying together *all* of the meanings I've heard in Don's famous quote over the years. Twenty years is a long time to do anything, especially being a chairman of the board. But eighty quarters is actually longer than twenty years because of the constant struggle to find the necessary balance in it all. In the end, you can't focus exclusively on the long term any more than you can on the short term. If I could ask Don today which is more important, I suspect I would get a response as simple—and enigmatic—as the one I've been decoding over the past fifteen years.

Both.

Figuring out how to balance both, and do it really well, probably will take me an eternity, or eighty quarters, whichever comes first.

CHAPTER 4

Help People See What They Want to Be

Anonymous

A few years ago, my boss was recruited to be CEO of a well-known multibillion-dollar manufacturing company, and he asked me to follow him as his executive VP of operations. Our mandate was to professionalize the company, which had gone public only a few years earlier, after many decades as a family-owned firm.

My role—a new one for this organization—presented an interesting challenge because I had functional responsibility for operations but the majority of the resources didn't report directly to me. Manufacturing was all done within three major SBUs, each headed by a president. Nonetheless, my specific mandate was, "Go fix operations. Make it better."

My boss offered his full support. "I want to get this done fast," he said. "We need to make improvements, and you have my backing.

The identity of the storyteller, as well as those of companies, other people, and locations in the story, has been disguised. Any similarity to actual people or companies is coincidental.

If people aren't doing things, tell me, and I'll make sure they do them."

His offer brought to mind the mantra from Don's class that's always resonated most with me—the one about power and authority. Relying on your power, he said, is like having one bullet in your gun. Once you shoot it, it's gone. If it doesn't get the job done—and I knew from my experience as a military officer that it often doesn't—you lose the ability to persuade and change people's minds. If they comply, they're only doing it because you made them do it.

So I opted not to take that approach. I decided not to set up a big corporate initiative for ops improvement and, using my boss's authority, force everyone to participate. I'd seen that in a previous company, where the emphasis seemed to be more on getting ops units certified than on real improvement. That was a "Here's the hammer—show me a nail" approach, and it got minimal compliance at best.

I worked two key success metrics out with my boss. First: 5 percent real annual productivity improvement as measured by cost per standard hour. That was the cleanest, clearest measure and was real dollars he could track and use to improve EBIT for the company. Second: participation. It needed to involve a wide swath of the company and not just a pilot in one or two locations. For myself only, I added another test. If my approach was working, people in the company would be coming to me and asking for help.

I had a vision of what needed to be done, but it was less specific than "Do A, B, C, and then D." I'm a big proponent of lean manufacturing, but my view of lean is simple and maybe even unorthodox. It comes down to two things: increasing the velocity of what's done—whether it's moving products from start to finish faster, reducing cycle time, or improving velocity of working capital—and variability reduction. Unless the customer is willing to pay for it, like a customized part, variability is waste. From those two principles, I can talk about most aspects or types of lean operations.

Taking a flexible approach based on these principles meant I could deal with each factory based on its own needs. The solution in one factory might be different from the solution in another because their situations were different or their products were made differently—a build-to-stock, seasonal operation versus a build-to-specific-design operation, for example.

The CEO shared my reluctance to create a big initiative. But more than once he told me, "When you figure out what needs to be done, tell me and I'll make sure it gets done."

And I kept pushing him back and saying, "I don't think that's going to help me be effective here."

The approach I took was more diplomacy than anything else. I approached each of the SBU presidents and got their blessing to deal with the ops people in their units. No one refused, but they did react differently.

One of the businesses, I'll call it SBU A, with an annual revenue of close to $2 billion, made equipment for the home market in four North American plants.

SBU B, with an annual revenue of $1 billion, made equipment for the commercial market in six US and European plants.

And SBU C, with a revenue of $800 million, manufactured made-to-design equipment in plants around the world.

All three SBU presidents knew that the CEO backed me, so none refused to let me work with their plants. None begged me to work with them, either. But one, the head of SBU A, seemed most receptive. He alone among the three lacked any ops experience, and I knew he was under pressure to make improvements. The head of SBU C was more or less neutral. And the head of SBU B, the commercial business, who had been a plant manager himself at one time, basically said, "Thanks, but no thanks." He thought I should fix everything else first because his plants were already world class.

I couldn't start everywhere at once, so I focused first on SBU A. I called the manager of the key plant there—it also happened to be the company's flagship plant, which was also a factor in my decision—and arranged to spend the best part of a day with him and his key staff.

The plant manager, who turned out to be a great guy, was naturally wary at first. He was in an awkward spot. He couldn't say no—he knew I worked for the CEO—but of course he didn't know what I was really up to. I'm sure he wondered, *Am I being evaluated?* or *Where's this going to go?*

I showed up and the first thing they wanted to do was show me all the metrics of how good they were. But I said, "No, thanks." I preferred to spend time on the plant floor. In fact, we spent the entire morning, seven thirty until lunch, walking around. Later, someone told me I was the first person from corporate who actually went out to a production line and spent time walking around. Everyone before me had spent twenty minutes riding around on a golf cart.

I spent the time not only because I wanted to gain some credibility but even more because I had relevant production experience and I wanted to understand what they were doing and how they were doing it. I took the opportunity to ask lots of questions. For example, they talked about how lean the plant was, and we came to a section where they were stockpiling a particular premade part.

"How many units are here?" I asked.

"Around one hundred thousand."

"How much production is that?"

"Well, it's a month."

"What happens if you find a leak in some of the parts because you had a problem with one of the setups? How many do you scrap?"

"Well, scraps are a little higher than we'd like."

At another point, I talked to a production line supervisor.

"What do you do all day?"

"Mostly I go looking for parts."

"Is that a good use of your time?"

"It keeps the line running."

"What if all the parts were here and you could work on improving ergonomics or quality or training your folks? Is that what you really want to be, a parts runner?"

"Well, I never thought of my job as a parts runner."

In the afternoon we all sat down, went through the numbers, and talked about what metrics they used. In some cases I pointed out how they were hiding problems by combining things. I knew how to do that because I'd done it myself and said so, and they began to realize that I actually knew something.

They also began to see that I was there to understand, and my ultimate motivation really was to help them. It wasn't a game of "Gotcha!" And I wasn't going to go back and report what I'd uncovered to the president or the CEO.

Part of that was personality, a little bit who I am. There's a way to do an ops review without making someone feel like you're just drilling him to make him feel like an idiot.

Finally, we reached the point of discussing overall performance, and it became clear that they hadn't improved productivity in ten years. When I pressed on this a little, they basically said, "We're not getting worse."

"Is that what you want to be?" I asked. "The 'we're-not-getting-worse' guys? Is that what excites you when you talk about the plant? Do you go to your kid's career day at school and say 'I work in a manufacturing plant, and our motto is "We're not getting worse"'?"

On paper it's hard to tell, but in person I have a sense of humor and can say these kinds of things in a playful rather than a sharp way that makes the point without belittling anyone. You open their eyes—but not in a nasty, confrontational way—to the fact that they're accepting levels of performance that they shouldn't be.

"Is that the best we can do, guys?"

At this point, after the tour, after the metrics, after we'd all gotten to know each other a little, we arrived at the most important part of the day when I could ask, "What do you really want? What are your goals? To be one of *IndustryWeek*'s top ten plants in America? To move manufacturing from a necessary evil to a competitive weapon? To make any product in any configuration and then load it on trucks instead of putting it in distribution warehouses for several months? That would be powerful, wouldn't it? Well, why don't we set that as our goal?"

These were good people, and I knew they wanted to be more than just the guys who made the products and hit the numbers.

"We don't know how to do that."

"That's OK. We'll figure it out."

Now they were thinking, *Wow! We can get better. We can be more than the guys who didn't hit the shipments each day.* And that led to talking about how to approach the challenge and what needed to be done—what they *wanted* to do.

A big part of the role I was filling was to be the advocate for operations. No one else on the executive team was playing that role. No one else was saying, "Let's think about how operations can add value to the company and what that would look like." Manufacturing is the profession where you almost never make anybody happy, especially in a company like this that's sales driven. You're always behind somehow. There's quality issues, delivery issues, and cost issues. I've never been in an organization where they celebrated the manufacturing guys for saving the day. It's a thankless job. No one ever says, "Thank God you guys are here!"

Finally, we reached a point where the plant manager, Tom, said, "Sounds like we're just coasting along. I don't want the perception to be that I'm a plant manager who coasts along."

"Tom," I said, "I'm not going to tell anybody that. That's not my motivation. My motivation is to help you be the guy who's leading the change."

"So you're really not here to assassinate us. You're not here to rip us a new one. You're really holding up the mirror and saying, 'Is this the best we can do?'" At that point, I think he turned a corner. "All right," he said, "how do we get there? I can't afford to make big investments."

"If I can help you get the resources you need so that it's not on your cost, would you be willing to work with me on this?"

"Yes, if you're telling me it's free."

"Well, it's not free to the corporation. It's an investment. But you have to sign up for the results. If the results aren't there, and the corporation's made the investment, you're going to have a little problem. I need you to be in."

And then he bought in. His sign of commitment was that he took his best operations manager off the production line and dedicated him to this project. That told me he was serious.

That's when we started to work together. I brought in three or four consulting firms that specialize in this work, and we selected one. And that's when it started to take off.

From there my involvement became checking in and asking, "How are we doing? Are we making progress?" It wasn't my role to help them lay out a production line. I wanted to make sure we weren't going in directions that weren't productive or not aligned with where we ultimately should get to. Overall, it took about nine months to a year—fairly typical. And it wasn't a single event. The first pilot was in three or four months, and when that was done, we transitioned to the next line.

It had a good outcome in a couple of ways. We got the 5 percent productivity improvement, the key goal, and the CEO began pressing the other SBU presidents to do the same.

The changes were well accepted in the plant too. We had forklift drivers, union members, bidding to go back and work on the production line. That was unusual because driving a forklift is usually one of the most sought-after jobs. You're not highly supervised. You get to drive around. It's considered a cool job. It was a telling point when these guys started to say, "I want to go back and work on the production line, because I want to see the units made right." The line was actually an easier job than driving, because it had been redesigned to minimize moving, lifting, and turning. So they could actually make something and get that sense of ownership, as opposed to moving parts around, and it wasn't something that killed you every day.

I got involved with SBU C because, after one of the executive meetings where we reviewed progress in the first plant, the SBU president came up to me and said, "I like how you're approaching it. We need some of that." And he became a real advocate—almost too much of an advocate. He was telling his people, "Do what he says," which wasn't quite the role I wanted, but we worked it out. We started with a plant they were moving to a different state, and then we went on to plants in Europe, which can be tough, but we had real success there too.

SBU B was the most interesting. The president was the only one with experience running a plant at this company. When the CEO pushed him to do what we were doing in the first plant, he said, "OK, if they're getting five percent, we'll get ten percent, and we'll do it by ourselves, and we'll do better."

That was what he said. What actually happened was that his plant manager called me and said, "I need help. But I don't want Jack (the president, not his real name) to know I'm asking for help. Why don't you come visit us?" I did, but he was nervous enough that for six months we wouldn't meet on the plant premises. Instead, we'd meet at a Starbucks far away in the city so I could review his slides or talk about his approach and what he was planning to do. Ultimately, I did go out to the plant, and we made a transformation very similar to what we did in the first plant. And they actually hit their goal of ten percent productivity improvement.

In the end, we eventually did lean initiatives in just about every plant, and we hit our productivity improvement targets. One of the SBUs actually declared that they thought of it first. I've always thought that when a group says they thought of it themselves, it's probably a pretty good sign of success.

I think it worked as well as it did because, going back to what Don said, if I had just used my authority, or the CEO's, to push through a big corporate initiative, we would have gotten minimal compliance, and maybe even malicious compliance, because it was just the boss telling people what to do. As I said, one of my personal measures of success was that people started saying, "Hey, when can you come help me? I like what I saw you do for him. I'd like some of that myself."

What worked was listening, understanding the specific situations and what people were trying to achieve in their businesses, the segments, and then working out the best way to modify the factories to improve their productivity within that environment. The approach was, "If you follow these principles, we're going to get productivity improvement." Five percent was not a goal. I talked about it with the CEO, but I never told anybody about it as we were working the changes. It became more, "Gee, if we do these things, we'll get better." My approach was to help people see what they wanted to be and walking them through that, as opposed to telling them what they needed to be and exercising my power to say, "You will do it my way." As Don used to say, that's one bullet, and when you shoot it, it's gone.

CHAPTER 5

Be Yourself

Denise Johnson

M y entry into manufacturing began immediately following graduation from LGO. Working in a factory for one of the major automak-
ers contrasted dramatically with my previous experience with the firm
in product development, affectionately named "the country club" by the
factory managers.

Many of the company's automotive factories were built in the 1920s
and 1930s, and they were dark, dirty, and extremely noisy. The plant
where I worked had been built in the 1940s, and, like all the plants, it had
a long history of male leaders and very traditional manufacturing management. For a male leader in this environment, especially one who had a
lot of time under his belt, the effective style in general was command and
control, often expressed by yelling louder, swearing profusely, and kicking
trash cans. That was what people had grown to expect from manufacturing leaders and plant managers.

I was one of the few women leaders in manufacturing, and, as a
woman in that environment, I quickly realized that I wasn't going to be
able to compete by copying that leadership style. I remembered one of
Don's mantras: "Be yourself. The number of effective leadership styles is

limitless." If I was going to succeed, it had to be with my own approach, which wasn't the traditional approach in that setting.

As a leader, I was highly focused on results and on the process for obtaining results. I made clear that we were going to hit our targets and hold people accountable. But I always tried to do that in a way that brought people along. That was my style. And, in contrast to traditional leaders in those plants, I spent a lot more time with people and a lot more time listening.

I started as superintendent on the night shift, and people noticed, even though I had young children, that I wasn't afraid to work hard. I came in early and stayed late. I developed programs to track the causes of frequent downtime so that we could address our key maintenance issues. I spent time talking with union officials to resolve problems and listening to workers' concerns and ideas.

I focused on results, and the hard work paid off. I moved from night shift to a lead role on the day shift. My responsibilities increased from superintendent to area manager to assistant plant manager. I remember feeling deeply honored when, finally, after eight years in manufacturing, I was named plant manager. I was the first woman in that position at this flagship facility, a 2.5 million-square-foot operation that built fifteen hundred full-size crew-cab pickup trucks a day in three shifts with a unionized, 90 percent male workforce with an average seniority of twenty years.

Plant manager was a demanding job. In a normal day, you came in extremely early and were there at least twelve hours. The line started at 6:00 a.m., and so you got in a half hour or more before that, headed out on the floor, and made your rounds through the entire facility, which took at least forty-five minutes, just to make sure everything was ready to go and to resolve any big issues that had come up. Then the rest of the morning you spent in standard meetings to gauge progress on various programs and issues.

As I stepped into this new role, I worked hard to fully implement lean manufacturing, using the principles I had learned at LGO and from Don. We focused on standardized work, waste reduction, and built-in quality initiatives. Working with my leadership team, we outlined clear expectations, drove process discipline, and recognized our team when we had great results.

Again, our hard work paid off. The plant won the Gold Quality Award for best-in-segment quality and was named one of the top three most efficient truck plants in North America by *The Harbour Report*. As a plant manager, I couldn't have been prouder!

Then the economy went into a downturn. Gas prices rose dramatically, and demand for crew-cab full-size trucks plummeted. Volume dropped so rapidly that the company had to rationalize its product footprint. Within six months the decision came from company leadership to reduce our plant from three to two shifts, then to one shift, and then—closure.

It really was hard for people to understand because, of all five truck plants then in production, ours was the one chosen to close, even though we had the highest quality and the best efficiency. Unfortunately, because of labor agreements, wages, and currency, we were also the highest cost.

Leading a team through such unexpected and dramatic chaos was not something I was trained to handle. I worried that my team and workers would feel betrayed by me because, as the leader, I represented the company and its decisions. It's devastating to hear that you're going to lose your job—remember, the average employee had been at the plant for twenty years—and I was the one who had to tell them.

We did all we could. We partnered with the union in asking, "What can we do to help people now that things are what they are?" We proactively worked to find new jobs for employees. We opened a transition center and staffed it full time with reassigned employees. The center included such services as counseling, resume-writing classes, interview training, and government agency contacts. We conducted job fairs and assisted in job searches throughout the greater metropolitan region.

In addition, we stepped up our communications. We wanted to be transparent in sharing what was happening and how we were planning to respond. Staying close to union leaders helped because, I heard later, there were some key individuals who at various times, after I had left for the day or even after I had left the room, would vouch for the fact that I was telling the truth and that I was doing everything I could to help.

Of course, we still had to maintain quality and process and keep things running smoothly. Even though the plant was going to close, we still had six more months to build trucks, and customers of those trucks expected the same high-quality product we had always delivered. So we talked every day about leaving our legacy in every truck that rolled down the assembly line.

But I would say those issues were more in the background, especially in the beginning. The moment we heard the plant would close, I realized that I would need to shift focus as the leader. Before, I concentrated on results and process and on people. But when the announcement came, my focus shifted primarily to people while monitoring results and process. We first needed to take care of people's immediate needs, and that meant not just answering their questions and helping them find new jobs; it also meant helping them get past their initial shock and anger.

I decided to cancel our traditional process-focused meetings that lasted from midmorning through the afternoon every day. Those were mostly future planning sessions. Once we knew the plant was closing, we didn't need them any longer. Instead, we would spend the majority of our time out on the factory floor, being physically present and visible to the workforce, talking with employees—employees who were working, employees who were on break—and, most of all, letting them share their emotions.

I didn't really change how I led or interacted with people. But I was physically and visibly present probably twice as many hours each day as I had been previously. I was there. People saw me. And it was comforting to them.

Even I was surprised at people's reactions. While they were shocked by the news, they wanted to talk about what was happening to them.

And it wasn't only me. I had the whole management staff do the same. I told them, "Just stay on the floor and talk to employees." Most managers in the plant were traditional, and it wasn't intuitive for them to do that.

Many of them just wanted to get away. "Let's make the announcement," they would say, "and then retreat." It was especially hard for them to deal with some pretty militant union personnel. The conflict and the anxiety levels were high. So their tendency, which I understood, was to go into a conference room and talk among themselves about what was next and what they needed to do—not to be out there in force themselves. I absolutely had to push them to do that in the beginning.

There was also a significant amount of coaching and discussion too. We talked about how to be approachable and empathetic. How do you look at someone as they're talking to you about their concerns? Are you taking notes? Are you taking their concerns seriously? Are you following up with them afterward? Are you showing empathy in the way you display your face, your posture, your openness to receive the message? Are you giving them a hug if they need a hug?

The hardest moments were when people cried. You knew they had families, mortgages, children in college. They knew their standards of living were not likely to ever be the same. They thought they might lose their houses. The chance of finding a job with the benefits and pay they were making in this facility was not high.

It was also difficult when they got mad, especially when they blamed. "It's your fault! It's the company's fault!" They wanted to find someone to hold accountable.

When this happens, the tendency is to defend yourself. But we found the better way to handle it was not to defend. Just listen. Nod your head. In some cases, come back afterward and say, "I thought about what you said, but look at it from this perspective." Or, "This is what's happening, this is what's going on. I appreciate your anger, but at the same time I want to talk with you about what I think is really happening." But not react immediately.

That was where I saw many of the male leaders struggle the most, because their tendency was to fight back. That's how they'd been taught. You come back at them with a counterargument. The person with the bigger stick is the one who ends up winning, or the louder voice, or the larger physique. Who's going to back down first? That was ingrained, I think, in the manufacturing culture, especially for males. So to respond in a different way, by not trying to retaliate, by listening, by coming back in a calm and collected way—I think that definitely was the way to handle those difficult situations.

Then, when people were ready, you tried to provide as much explanation as you could of what was going to happen next. It might be helping them write a resume or reviewing all the things that you do when you're starting to look for a job. You might even help them contact a counselor if you thought they needed help at a deeper emotional level. The idea was to get people past the shock and into acting in a way where they could see that their lives would go on and that there would be something more for them once they left the facility.

In spite of their initial reluctance, my leadership team learned to take this different approach. Once they had done it for a while, they realized it was the right thing. As soon as they got themselves into that mode, it didn't take much forcing after that. They bought in. They recognized the impact it was having on the people.

Over the next six months, the plant continued to build trucks, and quality stayed at all-time high levels. On the last day of production, we held a celebration—a funeral of sorts—to recognize all the men and women who had worked so hard over the years. We invited all of our retirees and previous employees to join us for the celebration. Thousands of people came to cheer as the last truck rolled off the assembly line. There were tears, hugs, and many memories shared that afternoon. As a final act, we placed every employee's name in a big tub. I had the honor and privilege of selecting the name of the employee who would be given the last truck ever built in the plant. It was an emotional day!

I'm sometimes asked if I took the approach I did because I am a woman. Was it a diversity thing? I don't think people looked at me as a mother figure but as someone who wasn't afraid to care or show she cared. To just listen, be there, be empathetic, show concern. That's not necessarily a female thing. But I think, in this environment, it wasn't something that they were used to. If a man tried to do the same thing, it could have still worked. But I don't know if it would have been considered genuine. I had an advantage because people didn't instantly assume that I was trying to manipulate them. It was genuinely the way I was. I had been there for a while before the plant closed. I was part of the team, and I had built a reputation, and people trusted me.

One of Don Davis's key messages applies well here: "Diversity in an organization is not only legally required and socially desirable, but it is effective." I don't know if what worked here was male-female diversity or simply diversity of approach. I do know that the traditional yelling, cussing, kick-the-trash-can style of management wouldn't have gotten the plant through those six months.

Another of Don's mantras also applied: "People lead people." Whatever made it work, tending to people as they worked through the shock and anger was an important step.

Don had so many pearls of wisdom about how to handle situations and treat people. What I remember most about him was that he was always a reflective leader. He was not one who was quick to anger. He was not one who was quick even to act when waiting was the better thing to do. He was one to be very thoughtful and deliberate in how he led teams. That always resonated with me as I listened to him speak. He wasn't an emotional leader, even though he could elicit emotion from his followers. He was a steady, secure, even stoic leader who people wanted to follow because he handled himself in a calm way and had a clear vision of where he wanted to take his team. To me that was always something I wanted to emulate. When I listened to him, I would think, *That's the kind of leader I want to be. Those are the kinds of things I want to try to copy from his style.*

CHAPTER 6

Trust, Leadership, Teamwork

Michael "Mick" Farrell

I was on vacation with my family in Sedona, Arizona, when I realized what I had to do. It was Monday, the first day of our spring break week, and I'd gotten up early to go for a run while my wife and our two kids were still sleeping. There was something special about waking up with the morning sun shining on those red rocks and the way it made them glow bright like the embers of a fire. As I ran through that gorgeous landscape, I suddenly said to myself, *That's it. I have to make this change, to light this fire that needs to be lit, as soon as I get back to the office.* It was something I'd been wrestling with, but now it was like an epiphany, now I just knew.

I was less than a year into a new role as president of North and South America for a billion-dollar-plus global medical devices company. I had profit-and-loss responsibility and ran all commercial functions for the two continents, constituting over 55 percent of the global sales for the public company. It was an exciting new role, with challenges I was eager to take on, in particular getting even closer to customers, driving growth, and improving more patients' lives.

Whenever I take on a new leadership role, I think about the lessons I've learned from the mentors and teachers in my life and how I might apply

STOP

them. A big part of that review for this position was recalling my time at MIT and the teachings of Don Davis. I pulled out material from his leadership course, circled some key words—I remember *trust, leadership, teamwork* in particular—and thought about what I wanted to do as a leader, the direction I wanted to pursue, and how I wanted to pull the team together.

Teamwork was critical. I wouldn't say my new team was falling apart when I arrived, but there were clearly many different silos. Sales had deep divisions with marketing, while marketing was split into five different subgroups—a traditional GE-type model where each separate function and subfunction did its work and they all reported to a single boss.

I wanted one team of partners focused on one thing: growth. I wanted to break down the silos, so I pushed all the groups to do three things together. First, set a strategic direction that everyone would sign up to and be inspired by: a big, hairy, audacious goal. I wanted us all to agree on where we would be in three years and five years and to really focus on numbers and specifics. Working together, we chose a goal of $1 billion in revenues for the Americas and a target of changing seven million lives by 2015. Second, have the whole group put their own team tactics together for reaching those goals that everyone could get behind: more than 50 percent of the strategic planning process is simply getting everyone on the same bus. And third, execute the strategy as one unit working together.

The second step, crafting a strategy and getting everyone behind it, was where I ran into a problem. The first part of the challenge was figuring out how we were going to reach the big, audacious goals we'd set, and the second part was getting everyone on the bus and moving forward together.

I felt like the school bus driver who was watching the road, while behind him, in the corner of his eye, he could see everyone throwing things, wrestling, and writing graffiti on the seats. But as soon as he turned around to look, the misbehaving would stop. If he said anything, everyone would point to someone else. Then, when he returned to focusing on the road ahead, it would start all over again.

I could sense something was wrong in my group, but I couldn't put my finger on it. Whenever I asked questions, people would say everything was fine or, as I said, they'd point fingers, though much of the finger-pointing did originate from one particular functional group. For example, when we began the budgeting process, I was dumbfounded when the VP of sales opened the first meeting by launching an aggressive attack against a key commercial program in another function. Right out of the gate. I thought, *Something's wrong with the team dynamic when the first conversation is an attack on an internal group as opposed to an attack on the competition or some specific business challenge.* Yet when I asked people about these kinds of incidents, no one would even admit they were problems.

Another example, the canary in the coal mine, suggested there was a problem in the sales group. Every year we'd take the top sales and clinical team performers and their spouses to a nice resort for a week as a performance incentive and as a way to say thank-you to the best of the best in our field team. We'd have an important meeting at the start of the first day, an open forum where the sales team could ask management—including the CEO, the Americas president, and leading research-and-development executives—any question, no holds barred.

When I have held such open forums with other functions, they're jam-packed with question after question—tough, detailed questions—about anything and everything. For this meeting, we scheduled an hour, but after ten to fifteen minutes of very generic questions—silence. Nothing. Crickets. I'm scratching my head. It couldn't be that no one had any more questions. Good people—and these were the best-of-the-best sales leaders in the Americas—always have questions. It was as if everyone was afraid to say anything. I asked myself, *Where's the trust gone?*

I was so worried, I sat down that evening with a group of regional managers and sales reps and said, "Look, what's going on?" I did the "5 Whys." No matter what the answer was, I asked, "Why?" and kept asking "Why?" Our work with Shoji Shiba at MIT in 1998 reviewing TQM and the Toyota Production System demonstrated that this rule of thumb ultimately gets you to the truth, or at least to the heart of the matter, when you get to the fifth why.

Even that wasn't working, and I was greasing the skids with fast-flowing tequila! Slowly, the group melted away until it was just me and one sales rep. I kept asking the questions because the nonverbal signals suggested there was something he just wasn't saying. It reminded me of the drinking bout in the Himalayan pub in the movie *Raiders of the Lost Ark*—see who falls off the stool first. This fellow did not want to crack. I was convinced there was something there, and I was determined to stay with it until it came out—and the tequila wasn't half bad either.

Finally, it worked. "Listen," he said. "Promise me what I tell you won't go any further." I promised, knowing that if he had to start with that request, this was going to be a very important conversation, but also knowing that the fact he needed to say those words rang alarm bells regarding the trust quotient I had assumed was in our sales management team. What I then heard were details and incidents of how trust was broken two levels above the field sales people—at the level of the area VP and his boss, the VP of sales.

I was surprised because the VP of sales was very effective at communicating upward and was also charismatic, empathetic, and able to connect with people and present reasonably well. He made you feel there was a lot of affection there. But the story that emerged told a different tale; it seemed the affection may have been just an affectation.

I understood how I'd extracted this information. It involved a lot of tequila and a president relentlessly grilling a sales rep—not necessarily an even fight. So I didn't take immediate action. I believed I'd heard someone courageously telling the truth as he knew it, but there was always the chance he was playing his own political game or just telling me what he thought I wanted to hear. So, I kept a skeptical viewpoint until I had gathered further evidence, but the seed had been sown.

When I returned to the office, I began proactively probing for information in all key areas and at all levels of the organization. From many conversations over four weeks from the field to the office and beyond, I ascertained that what I had heard wasn't the ramblings of one salesperson high on tequila at a resort. In those four weeks, I discovered that I had a political cancer in my organization.

It was located in the sales group and specifically in three individuals—the VP of sales and two area VPs under him—all of whom had been in the team several years. These three had taken control of the sales force and made it their fiefdom. For them, it seemed that the fiefdom and the benefits they took from it were more important than the company, shareholders, and customers.

What did they do? They broke expense-reporting protocols by having an assistant purchase many thousands of dollars' worth of furniture for their offices and then signing off on it themselves, rather than having their boss sign off as a standard check and balance. They took extravagant "team-building trips" to plush resorts, not as a performance incentive and only with the innermost circle of their team. Encouraged to talk at a later point, a sales leader who had attended one of those meetings told me, "It was like watching somebody steal from their grandmother." It galled me that the company was helping them and giving them an opportunity to grow, while they guzzled expensive bottles of wine, stayed at five-star resorts, and told folks to keep it quiet. Worse, they let it be known that if word of what was going on got out, swift action would be taken.

Wasting money was bad enough, but there was more: business trust was broken. As an example, let's say we all had agreed on a strategy of heading north. But, for whatever reason served their purpose or because they thought they knew better than the entire team (they didn't), they wanted to head west. They'd tell the sales force to head west and say, "If you get calls from management or corporate, tell them we're heading north." There were some very loud and clear examples of this from one of the area VPs about regional sales meetings where teams were lost because they knew the bigger strategy was north, but here was their direct leader breaking ranks and saying, "Let's go west."

These guys weren't buying into the strategy, but they wouldn't own up to it and didn't have the guts to debate it on merit. They just broke protocol and broke trust and pursued what they wanted. Or they would disagree and get shot down with better data and analysis from the team that wanted to head north. So they'd say, "Great!" publicly and then go do what they wanted to do. They'd smile while shaking their heads inside and saying to themselves, *Screw you. We're going to do what we want anyway.*

Finding out what they were really up to took a great deal of probing. They had established a control structure. They even used the word *trust*, which really infuriated me. They would say, "We've got to have trust within our teams." They even started meetings with "the five dysfunctions of a team," the first word of which was *trust*, and talked about how important trust was: the irony was incredible, and everyone in the room felt it, except maybe the presenter. If you stepped outside their fiefdom, their "culture," or were disloyal, even if it was the right decision for the company, you'd be demoted, pressured, or put down. They might move you out of your current role, move you sideways, or put you in a corner for some phony reason. It wasn't about what was good for the company or the sales team—it was what was best for them. Stewardship, a key tenet of Don Davis, had been lost and perverted.

They had established this infrastructure around them. They had neither the respect nor the hearts and minds of their team. They just had their fear. Everyone knew that if they stepped outside the line, they would be crushed. The level of control these people exercised, the fear they generated, was so strong that even other departments were careful not to cross them or speak out. The opposite of trust is fear; that was where the sales team was.

But further down the sales force, I heard many voices say, "We need to change this."

We considered our team to be a twenty-three-year-old start-up in that we try to keep entrepreneurial ideas and openness alive in all we do. We tried to think as if we were in mile one of a 26.2-mile marathon. We had still reached only 15 percent of the patients who needed our products in our most-developed countries; in developing countries, 95 percent of the opportunity was still in front of us. We were doing truly good things for the world, literally helping people stay alive. And here were some rogue sales leaders sending field agents out in the wrong direction, wasting money, and destroying what we'd built up over two decades. To have people tear it apart and prevent us from changing seven million lives by 2015, one patient at a time, just killed me.

As I thought about the problem, I kept returning to Don Davis's words, "trust, leadership, and teamwork," and his belief that leadership is stewardship. It's service. You do it for others, for some worthwhile purpose, not for yourself. "Selfship is the enemy of leadership." I remember him talking about stamping out self-serving politics when it emerges. And here it was. Selfship, pure and simple. It was a case study in self-serving politics from people who were supposed to be leaders and who should have known better.

I didn't look forward to what had to be done. I hesitated. Our culture is "work hard and play hard," and, to celebrate our success, it encouraged forming very strong ties with colleagues. Maintaining separation of church and state—keeping your friendships out of the workplace—was hard. I considered two of the three people who were in this group to be close colleagues, bordering on friends. As they say, trust runs away on horseback and comes back on foot. Confronting them would be some of the toughest conversations I'd ever have in my twenty-year business career.

The other consideration was that this was March, the end of the third quarter of our fiscal year. Fourth quarter was coming up, ending June 30, and that was the big year-end push, when sales teams hammer through. What would happen if I made these big changes in April? Would it destroy momentum and create so much turmoil and confusion that it stopped the big push? Not a small question for the company or for me.

There was a personal challenge here as well. I was president of the Americas, but I was also in the running for a higher position, and so my performance was being closely watched by the board. If I blew up the sales group by firing three key people, and everybody had to focus on picking up the pieces, I was likely to sacrifice the fourth quarter and maybe even the first quarter of next fiscal year. And that would probably sink my chances of the promotion. I wanted to think it through carefully.

I shared my concerns with some outside mentors who said, "You're doing the right thing by taking the action you've planned." One even told me, "The new team will rally behind you so quickly that your fourth quarter will probably be better than it would have been if you didn't make the change." I laughed because I didn't think that was possible. That would be the best-case scenario, but the more likely, worst-case scenario would be that the fourth quarter was out, the first quarter was out, and I was out of the running for a bigger job, dusting myself off, but having done the right thing.

That was when, by coincidence, I went to Sedona with my family for a week's vacation we'd already planned. In spite of the problems at work, I was trying to live the philosophy I'd also heard from Don of family first, then friendships, then company, and then giving back to the community.

It was there, in my early-morning run through those glowing red rocks, that I knew I had to move ahead and do what was best for the company as soon as I returned to work. *I'll do the right thing*, I thought, *and then I'll get the Americas division back on its feet before I figure out where I go for my next role. But I have to take the action no matter the consequences.*

At first my plan was to go back, sit down with HR, and then call the individuals into my office. I'd walk each of them through what I'd learned and tell them they had to come back and let me know what they were going to do to fix it. But as I tried to think three to five moves ahead like a chess player, I knew what would happen. There would be vast cover-ups. They'd go deep, and I'd eventually have to fire them. I had already informed them of the problems with trust that I had observed around strategy execution, so they'd had their warnings. We're told to hire with patience but fire quickly, and that's what I decided to do. This was a cancer and it had to be removed surgically, and right away.

Once I'd talked to HR and legal as well as my boss and my peers in the CEO's management team, I sat down with the three individuals, one by one, looked each in the eye and said, "Trust, leadership, teamwork. I can't trust you, and here are the examples where you've broken trust, including the north versus west analogy. Leadership. Here are several instances where you failed to exhibit stewardship, such as that skiing vacation the last week of the fiscal quarter. (The *last* week! Are you kidding me?) Teamwork. Here are multiple examples of how it was always about you and not the team or the company or the millions of people we're supposed to be helping."

None of the three admitted outright to any wrongdoing, but two of them admitted with their eyes. The other I felt sorry for because lack of self-awareness is a huge leadership liability. In the many months since they left, I've heard that two have moved on to new positions, but one has not. I've heard that one is still bitter, one not as much, and the other is right in the middle. If they learned anything about trust, leadership, and teamwork from the experience, then it was a good thing.

What happened afterward was incredible. I made the change on a Monday morning in April. The next day, my in-box was full of e-mails saying, "Good call," "Great decision," and "Right way to go," from people in the sales team and across the organization.

Not only that, but I watched the daily sales numbers pop up that same week, and they stayed up the next week and the next month. *What's going on?* I thought.

I called the outside mentor who had predicted this would happen. "I told you so," he said. "Look at who you promoted into those roles." This part was critical. The same day I fired the three people, I promoted new people into the three open sales VP positions. I sent out an e-mail announcement and held an all-hands conference call. The message wasn't about dismissals. Using the advice of a key board member, I turned the story around and talked about the company's code, focusing on the Davis mantra of trust, leadership, and teamwork. I thanked the three who were leaving for their service. Then I said, "Here are your new captains." The new VP of sales was very well known by the sales team and was also well respected because his group was already producing about half our Americas revenue in a role that required him to influence the whole sales team. The other two VPs had been part of an Americas leadership program that we had started with our corporate university just that year. The entire group rallied around the flag and their new leaders. The hair on the back of my neck went up when I heard the new sales VPs speak at their regional meetings and watched their new teams nod their heads: these weren't just good leaders, they were great leaders, who had already won the hearts and minds of their teams. At that moment, I knew that they would deliver, and we would deliver.

The results? Well, as you've probably guessed already, we hammered the fourth quarter. It was the biggest quarter in the history of the entire company for our team. We had a record year and the seventieth consecutive year-on-year growth quarter across the board in our organization. We finally had the strategy, the leadership, the ability to execute, and an entire senior team that believed in what they said and who also believed in trust, leadership, and teamwork. Not just saying it, but acting it. Talking the talk and walking the walk. We now had stewardship toward our purpose, our mission. We were now on the path to reach $1 billion by 2015 and to change seven million lives.

CHAPTER 7

Leave behind a Trail of Integrity

Anonymous

Ialways dreamed of owning my own business. In 2006, after working in the pet-care industry for a year, I saw a golden opportunity. High-end dog beds were a fast-growing sector of the market, but retailers couldn't stock an appropriate selection. There were no significant players online, and I saw the opportunity to rapidly carve out a role as the leading online retailer.

We grew extremely rapidly, from $400,000 in our first year to five times that—$2 million—in our second. However, while sales were growing, our bottom line was not, and we were broke.

We had raised initial money from angel investors, who gave us loans that would convert to equity when we found outside investors. Consequently, though the business had significant potential, I found myself on the hook for ever-increasing levels of debt, which rose to over $1 million. The stress of making payroll every week and the risk of literally losing our house was taking a toll on me and my family.

The identity of the storyteller, as well as those of companies, other people, and locations in the story, has been disguised. Any similarity to actual people or companies is coincidental.

I had lived through that nightmare myself already. My father had lost everything due to excessive leverage in his business—and I mean everything. When I was eighteen, we lost our house, my parent's marriage crumbled, and even money my grandparents had given me for college disappeared. I had seen the terrible toll financial distress had taken on my family growing up, and I had started my business resolved never to put my own family in that position—and yet, we were at risk.

I set my mind to raising equity from outside investors and made it my top priority. Almost immediately, I faced two dilemmas, either of which, I feared, could sour the deal we desperately needed.

First, I wondered how aggressive I should be in our financial projections. I wanted to be conservative, because I had been around long enough to know how hard it is to hit aggressive growth targets. But I also knew investors would greatly discount any projections we made. It didn't feel right for me to discount the figures and then for them to discount again—especially when it might mean they offered a lot less money for about a third of the company.

I made my decision based on reflecting on Don and his course, in which he had instructed us to be absolutely straight with our boards. His "only you can lose your integrity" maxim was in my mind as I dealt with this.

Instead of inflating the numbers, we based every piece of the forecast on what we'd actually demonstrated and on very reasonable and explicit assumptions about the market and what was changing in it. There was real substance to what we said.

In fact, when I reviewed the numbers with the investors they said, "Actually, you might be being conservative," which was, in retrospect, the perfect response. Too often they see naive and ungrounded forecasts, which only undermine their confidence in the team. What I learned was that their investment in the business was every bit as much an investment in me. When I was straight, the value of the entire enterprise went up.

The second issue in this A round of investment was keeping my promise to our angel investors. It often happens that institutional investors seek out ways to "cram down" angel investments. They say, in effect, "Look, we know what you were promised, but you're not going to get any money from us if you don't do this our way." It doesn't help that there are plenty of opportunities to shift value to institutional investors or to reward management with further stock options, without taking care of the angels. The angels do not sit at the negotiating table themselves, so the responsibility for defending their interests rested with me.

I viewed those initial investments as character loans. Many of our angels were friends and family, and I felt a very real obligation to them, apart from whatever legalities might be involved. For example, when one of our angel investors had sent me a check for over $100,000, he had not even asked for paper work. Instead, he said simply, "Treat me fairly." I wouldn't cash his check until I wrote down what that meant to me and sent it to him and the other angels for their review. I had promised them that the money they lent would convert to stock at a discount to what subsequent investors paid.

In fact, the A round institutional investor came in and proposed a structure that would advantage me personally but disadvantage the angel investors. I simply said, "No." I remembered Don's words about the CEO being a steward, and I considered myself a steward of the trust and money the angel investors had given us.

Fortunately, the A round investor understood where I was coming from and respected it. I believe that the respect he had for me probably helped close the deal when it nearly fell through for other reasons. My position did carry a cost: the investor's valuation of the firm was lower than it would have been under his original proposal. Still, I said, "Just treat it straight up. The value is the value." I never regretted that position.

We closed the deal, which took the debt off my shoulders and ensured at least a reasonably neutral outcome for my family financially if the business later ran into problems or failed. I remember taking my wife to a concert after closing the A round and literally getting tears in my eyes from the relief, once I had covered my family's downside and could breathe a little easier.

I'd like to think, even if I hadn't taken Don's class, that I wouldn't have lied, cheated, stolen, or done anything egregious. Having heard, though, from a guy who'd been through similarly tough situations and who'd come to believe in "building trust in all directions" as the foundation of everything else—that made a difference. It gave me the right place to start in sorting out tough issues when so much, including my family's welfare, was on the line. It gave me the confidence to move forward.

After securing the A round investment, we continued to grow dramatically. In 2008 our revenues rose fivefold again, to over $10 million, blowing away my more conservative projections. According to *Internet Retailer* magazine, that made us one of the fastest-growing online retailers in the world that year. Our growth actually continued after the financial crisis late that year, right through the first two quarters of 2009, when we were up 300 percent.

With numbers like that, I'm tempted to end the story here and say it all worked out wonderfully. But that wasn't to be.

Such rapid growth drove larger working capital requirements and soon led us to seek out a B round of investment. As we put together a deal, however, I began to grow concerned about our B round investor. My team's views of the company's future, how and where we should grow, differed from his views. I intuitively sensed that this could become an issue—actually, Don had told us how difficult it is to fix the problem when you and key stakeholders aren't in alignment on the fundamentals—but I didn't remember that until later.

I seriously considered killing the deal, but I didn't. The world financial markets had just cratered—this was early 2009—we were rapidly running out of cash, and I wasn't sure we could find another source of money quickly. I felt I had to protect the current investors—the angel investors and the institutional investor we already had—who had entrusted us with their money. Turning down an $11 million deal and risking running out of cash was not an option. If I had differences with the new investor, I decided, I would just have to suck it up, because my job was to make sure the company succeeded. We went ahead.

When it closed, the B round reflected a nearly threefold appreciation in the value of the company over a one-year period in which global financial markets had lost 50 percent of their value and small start-ups had fallen even further. The deal brought the company the money it needed and allowed some of the angel investors to fully or partially cash out. At that point, my equity was worth almost $10 million on paper. I had considered selling out in that round, but I didn't. The "great recession" had just begun, and I feared any discussion of leaving might sour the deal. Mostly, though, I stayed because I continued to be bullish on the company. We all looked forward to continued growth and success.

Then, in the middle of 2009 and only two months after the B round closed, there was a sea change in the competitive landscape. In 2008 Petco had been caught out of dog beds in the face of strong demand. Frustrated by complaints, Petco overreacted and bought far more beds in 2009 than it could sell as consumers cut back. It began liquidating dog beds at near and sometimes below cost. Not to be left behind, PetSmart, Walmart, and Sam's matched Petco's pricing, which kicked off a brutal price war in the category.

Worse, we had just launched an expensive new marketing campaign—at precisely the wrong time, it turned out. Our volume was up slightly that year, but pricing fell 33 percent, and we went from 400 percent revenue growth to a net decrease in revenues. We struggled to cut costs to match. By the end of the year, we were far below plan.

Excitement turned to disillusionment. Instead of the highly supportive and flexible board I'd enjoyed until then, my directors became aggressive and even threatening, with our newest investor leading the charge. Instead of relying on my judgment, the board insisted on dictating strategy that differed from the direction I thought made sense. I advocated broadening the business to include related products, while the board demanded an exclusive focus on cost cutting.

It got progressively worse through 2010 and 2011. I did focus on cutting costs, as the board directed, but it was not the strategy I wanted to pursue. We took more than 40 percent out of our overhead and were positioned for continued gains in efficiency, but our margins were still abysmal due to the ongoing price wars. We continued to lose money rapidly.

The one bright spot in this period for me was that my team stayed together. I'm proud that, in an industry with high turnover, in spite of the turmoil, we maintained almost zero attrition over a five-year period. I've been told that start-up boards will support founders, and some of their direct reports, but generally hate everyone else in the company. My experience certainly supported that view. I took lots of heat from the board in defending employees I believed in. But our team sensed my own commitment to them, and they remained highly committed to what we were doing.

Unfortunately, team loyalty couldn't overcome the fact that our strategy of focusing exclusively on dog beds was not working. We were making better margins than anyone else in the business by far, but everyone else was willing to accept a loss to drive foot traffic and sales of other products. Our gross margins simply would not support the overhead required to run our business.

Eventually, the market got so bad that Petco fired its own merchant, who had precipitated the price wars. But that was cold comfort for me because, by that point, due to missed forecasts, my personal credibility and stature with the board had suffered materially.

When I looked at myself objectively, I felt exhausted mentally and physically, worn down by the years of unrelenting pressure, and unable at times, I felt, to give the company the energy and engagement it needed and deserved. Though I still enjoyed my "day job" in an operational role, I began to dread dealing with the board. My family was suffering too.

After several discussions with board members over many months, I stepped down as CEO, and we agreed on a capable replacement. As I write this, though I'm no longer CEO, I remain a board member and a consultant paid to help with operations and, especially, with the sale of the business. The company is still in a very challenging market but is well positioned to survive and eventually recover and grow. Market pricing is recovering already. Though it isn't going to be a grand slam for the current investors, the company is in a solid position to make money for a new owner.

Why am I still involved? Given what the company is likely to fetch in a sale and the fact that my equity isn't preferred, I'm unlikely to get more than about 2 percent of the proceeds. So I'm not doing it for the money. In fact, it's incredibly painful for me to still be engaged. It is extraordinarily difficult to lose what you've built to others and then to work to make them successful.

But I'm involved because I still have a responsibility to help those who put money in my business—from angels to our B round investors—get every dollar they can. Honoring the deal and continuing to work, despite tough circumstances, to make our investors' exit a success are my current focuses—along with thinking through next steps for myself personally.

The experience certainly didn't turn out the way I or my investors had hoped. But it didn't cost me my relationship with my wife, my children, or my investors, and I live to fight another day. I've come out feeling proud of what I did and how I conducted myself. I've come out believing I did everything I could for the people who entrusted me with their money and their careers. In turn, I have retained the trust of a greatly widened network of colleagues.

Frankly, that's where the value is for me going forward. If I look at my own personal balance sheet, my biggest asset is that I came out of this with a whole set of people who will help me. Many are already helping me, and I'm already looking at an amazing set of new opportunities. Because of the way I operated, the way Don taught us, I get a chance to realize financial success the next time.

Many entrepreneurs fail in their first business and don't succeed until their second or third effort. The ones that burn bridges don't get a second chance. The only way you get to keep trying is if you leave behind a trail of integrity.

When I think about Don, I think about the person as much as the mantras. I think of the twinkle in his eye, how he made us all laugh, and how I grew to trust him. I don't think of the mantras as a set of twenty lessons or a to-do list. It's a practical guide for creating trust, which is the foundation of every effective business and every successful marriage. Don provided a ground-up perspective on how to build relationships and how my own conduct and integrity can help me achieve my goals and aspirations.

He taught us to always tell our board the truth—which I did unfailingly. He taught us to be selfless team players—which I did, and I'm extremely proud of that. He taught us to look for alignment of values with our board and investors—which I will definitely do a better job of next time. And he taught us—though I'm not sure I fully understood this before—that having a lot on the line doesn't change what you need to do. Having had somebody else insist on the importance of taking the right course—building trust in all directions—helped me navigate this very difficult period successfully.

CHAPTER *8*

Tell the Truth

Scott Pierce

At a meeting in mid-September, I heard that a $5 million progress payment from a major customer was late. It had been due on the first of the month, and we needed it by September 30, the close of the quarter, to meet our cash targets. Shareholder performance and executive bonuses—including mine, to some extent—hung in the balance.

I was working in the international sales department at an aerospace OEM. The customer was a large international organization headquartered in the Far East with US offices in Washington, DC. I had been the sales manager when I sold seven multimillion-dollar aircraft to this customer the previous year. Now, with those kinds of dollars at stake, I wasn't the only one who took notice.

The customer claimed we weren't abiding by a memorandum of understanding (MOU) linked to the sales agreement. The MOU obligated us to consider, among other things, making the customer a service center and spare-parts distributor in the Far East. Our aftermarket group had considered all the possibilities in the MOU and decided not to pursue them. The customer didn't like that decision and, in hopes of changing it, was refusing to pay. They had delayed two previous progress payments for the same reason, but each time they had finally paid by the end of the quarter—but just barely. Both payments had arrived on the evening of the final day of the quarter, one of them arriving just before the midnight deadline.

As days passed, it began to look like that might not happen this time. Payments weren't handled at my company by the sales group, and, in any case, I had since been promoted out of direct connection with the customer. But I still had close contacts there, so I called them to see what I could do. They said they were determined to reopen the MOU issues and wouldn't make any more payments until that happened.

With only a few days left in September, I realized that I was in the best position to collect the money because, in my previous position, I had developed closer ties with the customer than anyone else. So I called and arranged to see the key people in Washington on the last day of the month.

When the day came, I flew down in the morning, and we met that afternoon.

"Hey," I said, "we need this money. It was due a long time ago. It's in our financial plan. The aircraft are on final assembly, and we need a progress payment."

They wouldn't budge. "We're not making the payment," they told me. "Our boss won't let us make the payment. We wanted the service center and the other items. That has to get resolved first."

I left and called the office. "They're not going to make the payment," I said. "Sorry, guys. I have to go on to my next meeting," which was a dinner meeting.

After dinner I returned to my hotel and got a call from the customer, who asked, "What's going to happen if we don't make that payment?" We talked about the resentment it could cause and perhaps even the collapsed relationship between our companies. Through the evening there were maybe two more calls and brief discussions, but nothing that led me to believe they were going to pay. Then, late, another call: "Hey," my contact said, "I'm coming over with the checks." There were two checks totaling $5 million.

I got dressed, because I had already gone to bed, and went downstairs to the parking lot of the hotel, where I sat in my contact's car. "Well," he said, "we didn't want to make this payment, but we listened to what you had to say, and we think it's ultimately, in the long term, the way to go.

But we really want some traction on these other things. Please do what you can."

I grabbed the checks, went back upstairs, wrote a quick e-mail—"Got the checks!"—and went back to bed.

Next morning, the beginning of a new financial quarter, as I sat on the plane at the gate, waiting to return home, I got an e-mail on my Blackberry: "You have the checks? Where are they?"

"Yes," I replied. "In the overhead bin."

Two minutes later, a second e-mail: "When did you get them?"

Obviously, he was hoping I got them at 11:59 p.m. or sooner, before midnight and the close of the quarter. He didn't say that, and there was no pressure, but I knew what he wanted, what everybody wanted. I thought about it for five seconds and replied: "12:45 a.m."

I knew it had been only the customer and me in that dark parking lot, and I was sure the customer didn't care what I said. But I just couldn't lie about it.

Don had a part in that decision, but it wasn't that I was sitting on the plane, fingers paused on my Blackberry, and thinking back, "What would Don do?" I'm not sure in that moment I even connected the two. But living under the honor code at West Point and then going to Don's class, you internalized those standards. You saw this man with his set of values who was so successful in life and business, and you thought that was something to aspire to. He really had strong values, probably stronger than anybody else's I've ever met, stronger than mine, for sure. And I looked up to that. He told us to have values and to stick with them, not to let anybody or any situation take them away. Business or life, the same.

I heard a day or two later that the CFO had taken the checks into the previous quarter. He reasoned that they had been prepared before the end of the quarter with the intent of delivering them before midnight, because it would have taken that long to print them and drive them over to my hotel. So he basically booked them for the quarter that just ended, and we got the credit.

I'm fine with that decision. The logic makes some sense, and I'm no accountant, plus no one ever suggested I change my story, which I wouldn't have done.

I also heard later that what happened made it all the way up the chain to the president—that "Scott did his best, and this $5 million actually came through. He got it at 12:45 a.m., and he told us he got it at 12:45 a.m." I was pleased to hear that. Don said to have a code in business, to live by it and be known for it, and to beware the slippery slope of small compromises. Everything works better when people can count on each other to tell the truth.

CHAPTER 9

Only You Can Lose Your Integrity

Anonymous

It seemed a lifetime ago that I was sitting in Don's class, absorbing as much as I could from this man who not only put you at ease immediately but also emanated leadership. I remember thinking, as Don taught us how to deal with a board of directors, that this was surely a skill I was never going to need. Still, I listened intently. Don's faith in each of us boosted my confidence and actually had me believing that maybe, someday, I could be dealing with a board of directors.

In fact, I was working with a board only eleven years later—far sooner than I expected—and I was struggling. It was early January, and we were deep in preparation for the monthly board meeting. It was always my job as COO to report company results, but this time I had the added duty of presenting our budget for sales and expenses in the New Year.

The identity of the storyteller, as well as those of companies, other people, and locations in the story, has been disguised. Any similarity to actual people or companies is coincidental.

Mike, the CEO, and I couldn't agree about what to say. Mike had no use for the board at all, and board meetings were, at best, a necessary evil, something to get past so we could get on with business. So his goal for this meeting was to present a rosy forecast with confidence and enthusiasm. That's what board members expected to hear, according to Mike, and so that's what we should give them.

I didn't share Mike's view of the board or his desire to project an optimism that I felt was unwarranted. We had previewed the numbers in the December meeting and promised to present full details this month. I had held my tongue, but I wouldn't have that option this time.

This was the latest in a running struggle between Mike and me. I had been with the company less than a year, and what had started as my dream job was starting to unravel.

The company—Supplier.com—was a global online site where companies that wanted something made could find manufacturers with the necessary skills. Ten years old, Supplier.com had attracted about $50 million in VC money and built a sizeable marketplace. By some estimates, the dollar value of business transacted on or through our site made us bigger than eBay or other similar online marketplaces, even Amazon.

Mike was the founder-entrepreneur who lacked any real experience actually running a large organization. That was my job, and I had arrived with excitement about the promise of this venture. When I learned the ropes, I was told, I could replace Mike as CEO.

At the time, Supplier.com had some 325 employees at headquarters in Chicago and spread around the world—China, Germany, Switzerland, France, and India. Annual revenues of $30 million came solely from some five thousand manufacturers (the "sell side") that offered their services through our site and paid about $6,000 a year for the privilege. Buyers who needed something manufactured (the "buy side") paid nothing.

I had soon realized this was a problem. Results were trending down, and the company wasn't hitting its projections. Little analysis had been done before I arrived, so I placed high priority on digging into the data and understanding why this company that seemed to have an incredible business model was still losing money after being in operation for a decade.

I had been told the declining results were a "marketing problem"—that is, a problem signing up new manufacturers. But analysis said the problem was more fundamental. Most manufacturers were not reaping any real tangible benefit from the site, and so the vast majority—around 90 percent—were going away each year. These nonrenewers hadn't even recouped in gross revenue the annual fee they paid Supplier.com. Worse, we discovered that many buyers, since the site was free, were obtaining no-cost quotes through us that they used to beat down their regular suppliers. Finally, we couldn't even brag about the amount of total business transacted on our site. Buyers and sellers, once they found each other on Supplier.com, could transact their business, including any repeat business, away from the site.

Consequently, my executive team and I believed strongly that we needed to generate revenue from the buy side. But Mike felt strongly—with almost religious fervor—in the current model, which he had devised. He constantly made the analogy that Supplier.com was like a bar that offered free drinks to women whose presence would attract throngs of paying male patrons. The presence of buyers, for whom the site was free, would draw manufacturers and justify what we charged them. I understood the analogy, but in fact it wasn't working. In spite of Mike's opposition, I put together a team focused on figuring out how to generate buy-side revenue and improve the customer experience for the buy-side users.

That was only one of many problems with Mike. He and the board—which comprised Mike, representatives from two key investors, and the previous owner of another online marketplace Supplier.com had acquired—made clear they held me accountable for results, not Mike. Problem was, Mike not only involved himself in key decisions, but he did it sporadically and unpredictably.

To deal with our declining numbers, for example, I held a number of brainstorming and strategy sessions. Mike showed up for some but not others. When he did attend, he often tried to change the entire direction the team had chosen. For example, at one meeting we all argued that unless we invested in the buy side we would never have a value proposition on the sell side. Mike got so mad he stood up, left the meeting, and stormed off in his Ferrari.

We ran a program aimed at removing waste and improving the way our marketplace worked. Mike and the board strongly supported this effort. He even came and talked at a final, intensive, days-long working session we held with one of Supplier.com's major buyers. Then, when that program produced a set of recommended changes that everyone involved supported, Mike told the IT group not to implement any of it.

At one of the all-hands online meetings I held periodically for everyone in the company, I pressed the need to eliminate unnecessary costs and conserve cash. In his final comments, literally the last words everyone heard, Mike explained that his ideal company would be a website, him, and one other person to count the money. That, along with a number of other statements and actions, did not endear Mike to his employees.

By the time we were preparing for the January board meeting, I felt trapped and torn. I considered leaving, but I had convinced several key executives to leave good jobs and join Supplier.com. I thought, *Boy, if I quit six months after I've hired you, that is a real schmuck move.* If someone did that to me, I would feel betrayed.

Also, I had moved my family to Chicago. We'd moved many times, but my wife and I always said that, once our children reached high school, we would stay where we were. Our daughter had just started high school in Chicago.

When Mike adamantly opposed all the key changes we proposed, I realized my only alternative was to take my disagreements with him to the board. Yet that option seemed unlikely to work. The investors whose representatives sat on the board still viewed Mike as the brilliant entrepreneur-founder (or at least felt that they had no option other than Mike). In my periodic one-on-one phone meetings with those members, I found that they responded to any mention of problems with one retort: "You're responsible for the company. Fix it." In addition, I quickly discovered that anything I told them was immediately communicated back to Mike. Clearly, I could fully involve the board only if I launched an all-out mutiny, and I couldn't see anything good for the company coming from that approach.

Mike always involved himself deeply in board meeting preparations, especially one as important as the upcoming January session. He insisted on knowing and approving in advance everything we said to the board. As a result, the board only half-understood the reality of the company.

I had never been allowed by Mike to present the full results of the deep analysis we had done. Board members were aware of the number of manufacturers not renewing—the high-level numbers. But they didn't know the real reason, which was that the vast majority got no tangible benefit at all from Supplier.com. Members were being led to believe the problem was just a series of bad sales months. I pressed Mike to let me present what we'd learned to the board, to open the kimono about the real challenges we faced. He refused.

At the December meeting, we had presented preliminary year-end results, but those of us on the inside knew that information was less than complete or forthcoming. We had also presented the rosy preliminary numbers for the New Year that Mike had insisted on presenting. I considered them an unrealistic stretch. When Mike and the board tried to gauge my confidence in them, I'd avoided making any commitment. However, that would not be possible in the January meeting.

Several times through these trying months, I thought about Don Davis and what he would do in my predicament. Don's view of a board was diametrically opposed to Mike's. Don said to consider the board a partner and resource and to be as transparent and forthcoming with it as possible. Under Mike, of course, I couldn't apply that piece of Don's wisdom. But Don gave me something even more important than specific advice. He gave me the confidence to follow my own compass. I knew what was right and wrong because of the way I had been brought up. But Don gave me confidence to apply that compass in business. Because of Don I never doubted what I had to do. I couldn't and didn't resign, because that felt like reneging on commitments I had made to the company, my family, and those I'd persuaded to join me at Supplier.com. But I wouldn't lie about what I knew and believed.

I went into that January board meeting with Don in mind. We presented Mike's wildly optimistic sales projections for the New Year. But when the board asked what my level of confidence was, I said it was low—I considered the projections an extreme stretch. Also, when we talked about the previous year's results and I presented additional information uncovered by our deep analysis, I gave the board a much more frank appraisal of what was happening on our site and the experience of manufacturers using it. My candor did not please Mike.

Not long after that, I had a phone meeting with one of the board members. In spite of Mike's coaching, I opened up even more with this member about what we had found in the data, what was going on inside the company, and my low confidence level in the forecast that we had submitted. As usual, the board member told me it was my problem—"What are you going to do about it?"—and then passed along everything I said to Mike, who was even more displeased. That was probably the final straw for Mike.

Finally, in March, I went to work one day, just prior to that month's board meeting, and Mike called me aside. He had met with the board personally, he said, and they had decided the company couldn't afford a COO anymore.

I was both shocked and relieved. Again, Don's teaching came to my rescue. I was being pushed out. After a lot of success up to this point, this was my first professional failure. Most of what you're taught in a top business school like MIT is that you're perfect. You graduate thinking, "I'm bulletproof." But Don was the most honest voice in my graduate program. "Here's the reality of business," he said. "You will definitely make big mistakes in your career. The key is learning from them and moving forward and being honest about them and honest with the people around you."

Because of the perspective Don had given me, I was able to look back and learn a tremendous amount from my experience at Supplier.com, which clearly was a failure from a professional point of view. I should have moved much faster to address the financial and business-model challenges the company was facing. I should have spent less time traveling to company sites away from headquarters so that I could spend more time focusing on the process improvements that would turn around our operational results. Lastly, I should have spent more time building relationships with the members of the board, recognizing that to truly turn the company around, I was going to need their full support.

Without Don, I wouldn't have had the confidence in my own sense of what to do, I would have been crushed by the experience and the outcome, and I wouldn't have been able to benefit from the valuable lessons I learned.

CHAPTER *10*

Never Deal with Someone You Don't Trust

Anonymous

When we moved into our current house nine years ago, it was our tenth move in less than a decade. As I began unpacking once again the books, papers, journals, and articles I'd been carting around—the accumulation from my career, grad school, and college—I resolved to go through it all and figure out what was important. I devoted a whole weekend to reviewing *every* page and asking, "What is truly worth keeping? What is still useful and relevant to me where I am now?"

In reviewing thousands of pages, I came across a piece of paper from our class with Don. It was his list of leadership mantras. Though I'd saved it—and I certainly hadn't kept everything—I don't think I'd ever thought about it all that carefully when taking his class. I liked the class—there were some very profound learnings—yet I wouldn't say it had had an enormous impact on me at the time.

The identity of the storyteller, as well as those of companies, other people, and locations in the story, has been disguised. Any similarity to actual people or companies is coincidental.

Yet, in reviewing this piece of paper several years later, I was struck by what incredibly great advice it was. It seemed important and useful in a way I'd never realized before. I read a lot of management books and articles—*Harvard Business Review* and *Sloan Management Review*—but this seemed different. This was a person speaking at the end of a long life about what he thought was most important.

So I laminated Don's advice and put it up on the wall in my office at eye level—right where I would see it every time I sat down at the computer. Over these last nine years, as I've looked at it virtually every day, what it says has started to become etched in my consciousness and has had a profound impact on my life.

Don's comments about exercise and being with positive people have been important to me. And, at times, when I didn't want to do something, his mantra "Look for opportunities to practice leadership" seemed to apply. Because of it, I made a major career transition that took a lot of courage, because it was an unusual move to make.

As a consultant, I have worked at the highest levels of many large and small companies, with leaders whose decisions had great impact on business strategy, new products and markets, and on the individuals and groups in their organizations. Don's mantras on that laminated page by my home computer helped me understand and deal with problematic situations in two different organizations.

Both were similar in that the behavior of key leaders was inappropriate, I felt. No one was breaking the law. Instead, the main issues were around lack of transparency in the leader's dealings with investors, colleagues, and employees.

As I was involved with each of these situations, I would sit at my computer, and inevitably my eyes would be drawn to Don's words—"Leadership is service, stewardship based on trust" and "The ethics of an organization are no higher than that of its leader." And, of course, "Never deal with someone you don't trust."

What made it really hard was that both organizations happened to be among the most fun I'd ever worked with. They were young, growing groups making a difference in dynamic industries. The leaders were attractive and charismatic. I loved what I was doing, and I wanted to keep working with them.

But every day I would look at that piece of paper and ask myself, *If I don't believe this person is being ethical and straightforward with the individuals funding him or the people he's leading, then how can I work with him, even though he's charismatic and the work is exciting?* In both situations, I didn't want to face the problem for a long time. In each, I probably spent a month not sleeping well, wrestling with what to do.

In both situations, I ultimately decided to separate myself because I couldn't be part of something that felt less than honest or transparent. If the leaders weren't forthright about the company and what investors and others were getting into, how could I stay involved? I ultimately realized I could not avoid listening to this voice in my head—it felt like Don was counseling me, guiding me—and I had to leave those organizations.

In school, I understood what leaders do, but my perspective was more theoretical than experience based. I had never faced situations where I was in danger of losing my personal integrity. When I came across the mantras years later, I had more real-life experience. I'd made career decisions, seen a number of organizations, lost family members, and was just older. I was able to understand better what Don was saying.

I'm often struck by the gift of coming across that piece of paper from Don's class after all those years, that it resonated so much with me and what I'd learned since leaving school, and that it's had such a profound impact on my work and life. I'm glad I found it. Years later, it's still on the wall, and I look at it every day.

CHAPTER *11*

Leaders Lead People

Chris Richard

Two years after graduating from LFM, I took on a new role at a major semiconductor company as the global manager of industrial engineering for assembly and test manufacturing. My mandate was to transform how eleven separately managed groups of industrial engineers (IEs) collaborated on a global scale.

The problem driving this change was that the company was spending hundreds of millions of dollars each year on capital equipment without models and standards for performance that applied consistently across its various factories. Consequently, it was extremely difficult and time-consuming to compare and evaluate even routine capital equipment requests submitted by different factory managers.

Solving this problem meant I had to create an IE organization that could effectively perform two key tasks. First, we needed to accurately estimate what and how much new equipment each factory should buy months and years into the future. Second, we had to perform scenario analyses accurately and quickly. For example, we might get a question like this: "We're scheduled to produce twenty-five million of a particular product this quarter, but it looks like we can sell twenty-eight million if we can produce them. Can we do that?" The plants usually received several such questions each week.

At that time, the plants needed one to three weeks to respond, and even then the responses were hard to compare because of plant-to-plant variations in how the responses were prepared. If only one factory was involved, you could get an answer in a week; but if you had to coordinate across three, four, or five factories, it would take three weeks. That was far too long. The company needed answers in days, or sometimes even hours.

I began to tackle the problem by spending time at each plant to get to know the key employees. I already knew many of them from my previous role, but now I focused on identifying the expectations of everyone involved, the strengths of the current IE organization, the particularly strong employees, what was working well, and the obstacles that kept us from working more effectively.

I quickly discovered a major problem: there was no common, agreed-upon source of data—what we called the "plan of record"—for certain key equipment parameters, such as the number of units per hour that a machine would be able to produce of a certain chip nine months in the future. As a result, when a question came down—"Can we increase capacity?" for example—the IEs had to meet with key engineers and operations people to get them to commit to a number, data point by data point, one by one. That could take a week or two. Then, the IEs updated their spreadsheet models with the numbers to see if they met the need. If not, they had to go back to the same people and find a way to close the gap. Eventually, after two or three weeks, they would submit an answer.

I soon realized that one of the first things we needed to do was freeze the data rather than, for each request, ask everyone for their number. We needed a process in which the factories put their numbers in a database that they certified was correct, a store of data that they owned and kept current—that is, a plan of record for the key data.

No question, part of the solution was better systems, processes, and procedures. In fact, it would have been easy to diagnose and try to deal with the problems entirely in those terms. That's the way, I suspect, most managers would have proceeded—by imposing systems, processes, and procedures that put the company's corporate priorities first and the site's or factory's priorities second.

But one of Don's mantras was that leaders lead people. In this situation, I realized that if I did not recognize and deal with the *human* side of this situation, no amount of system, process, or procedure change would work for long. And that brought to bear another of Don's mantras—that it's important to know your people. I had to understand *why* people were doing what they were doing—and not just my IEs but their partners and stakeholders—and *how* to change that.

The company had built its first assembly and test site twenty-five years earlier in Penang, Malaysia. Then, over the years it had added additional sites, most in the Far East. When I began my assignment, the company was running fourteen factories in five countries, along with a development site in the United States, that all needed to collaborate as they managed technology transfer and manufacturing operations.

Each factory operated hundreds of millions of dollars in equipment and was adding more every quarter, both to handle higher volumes—the company was growing 25 to 30 percent every year—and to deal with the fast-growing complexity of the chips. In addition, the company continued to add new sites that needed equipment.

The company's manufacturing philosophy called for all manufacturing processes at all sites to run in exactly the same manner. That approach was essential, because the company's new processes included a number of variables that could create significant yield and production problems if they weren't precisely controlled.

Because the manufacturing philosophy was relatively new at that time to these assembly and test factories, there was considerable variation in the way different factories estimated and forecasted capacity. Some variation came from the fact it was always in a factory manager's self-interest to have a little more equipment than needed to hit a quota. Some variation arose from the inherent complexity of modeling, sizing, and controlling the constraints in a complicated, multistep manufacturing process. An even further variation arose from the efforts of individual IEs in different plants to constantly tune their spreadsheet capacity models to reflect local conditions and priorities.

These differences were the source of the major and growing problem we faced. How could the company introduce new and increasingly complex manufacturing technology? How could it plan for and allocate capacity across all its different factories, when each factory, over time, had evolved different ways of estimating its production capacity and equipment needs?

Given this background, it was clear that mandating a plan of record would be easier said than done. It would require all the engineers and operations employees to submit numbers, commit to them, maintain them, and, worse, to lose some control over them by making them transparent. I knew that my IEs and I couldn't make a system work if the operations or engineering people maintaining it didn't support the change.

The lever I did have—and I knew this from my travels to the sites—was that these proud teams of industrial engineers wanted to do their jobs as best they could. But, they often found themselves torn between local management and the manufacturing group's corporate priorities. Site allegiances were much stronger than ties to "corporate," not least because most decisions about individuals' careers were made at the site level.

In addition, the IEs had to deal with four or five major stakeholders on each site who often gave them conflicting directions. Besides the shot-calling factory manager, there were engineering managers who controlled how fast the equipment ran; operations managers who greatly impacted utilization; and planners who constantly negotiated the balance between supply and customer demand. So the IEs were in the middle, trying to balance what was right for the company, what was right for their local site, and what was right for them.

Two more factors made the IEs' work even more complicated. First, they tended to be more junior than their operations and engineering counterparts. As more junior employees, they lacked enough formal authority—an important factor in many of the local cultures, which revered positional authority—to secure the necessary commitments.

Second, the IEs' careers were mostly tied to the local site, not the company worldwide. The sites hired them and provided career opportunities well beyond those they might find solely within their IE organization.

So I couldn't build a castle wall around the IEs and tell them to follow corporate guidelines and ignore local pressure. That wasn't going to work.

To achieve my goals, we needed to find a way that IEs could stand up and hold their own in the local operation, make a genuine contribution to the operation and be recognized for it, and have a rewarding career.

As part of the changes we made, we did improve processes, systems, and tools extensively, but we also took a number of other crucial steps.

One of my first actions was to obtain formal reporting authority over the IE organization. I insisted on a dotted-line link between me and the IE managers, who began reporting to me in addition to their local factory manager. Matrixed management was a common arrangement in the company, but it hadn't been done before with the IEs. As a peer of their factory managers, I could counterbalance local priorities and advocate at the staff level for the changes needed.

Next, I pressed to standardize the grade levels and expectations of the IEs across all the different sites. Before that, their roles varied considerably. For example, in one region the IEs had been responsible for everything required to start up a new factory, including some aspects of construction, as well as hiring and training the direct labor force. I gave them all the same, more focused charter. In some sites, we had IEs who were too junior. They were well motivated and well intended, but they were several grade levels below their engineering and operations counterparts. So, we got the right people in those positions at the right grade levels. Part of this exercise included consolidating eleven factory-based IE organizations into five site-based organizations (all sites had multiple factories).

As a result, the IEs became what they really wanted to be—the third leg of a three-legged stool, the equals of their operations and engineering colleagues, and no longer the scapegoat if the factories missed their output goals.

Within the IE group, we worked with IE managers to explicitly define the vision and objectives shared by the entire IE group. That gave them a real sense of purpose, which was to maximize the amount of production and manufacturing volume the company could produce per dollar invested. They were the guardians of that investment and made sure it wasn't wasted. They were also keepers of the data, charged with making sure it was always up-to-date. And they were responsible for direct labor productivity—determining how many people were needed per machine per shift to keep the machines running. They didn't manage those people, but it was their analysis that determined how many people factories were authorized to hire. Finally, after clarifying their key roles and responsibilities, we established a common set of metrics for measuring IE performance.

Once a quarter, I brought together my central staff with the IE managers from the five major factory sites for a three-day workshop. At these sessions, we worked through defining our vision and objectives, conducted training, and covered other IE business. As a result of this intensive work, I identified a number of strong industrial engineers who could help with tools and processes that had to be driven centrally and who could coach, mentor, train, and develop the people in the distributed sites.

We had to upgrade their leadership capabilities too, so they could work more effectively with their counterparts in engineering and operations. For example, if an engineering manager said to an IE, "I need another quarter to get the test time down," we needed IEs with the strength, seniority, and expertise to say, "That's a major problem. We have to work through that." So we conducted training for IE managers around negotiation, peer leadership, and collaboration, with sessions as well around motivating, training, developing, and growing their own organizations.

We reinforced what we were teaching on the job. For example, we put together a customized survey tool that let all IEs receive individual feedback about how they were perceived by their subordinates, peers, and managers. Based on this and other input, every IE manager created an action plan for personal development that was then reviewed in a meeting with both me and their local factory manager. It was important for the three of us to do this together, because I didn't want the IE managers caught in the middle of conflicting objectives.

We performed basic career planning and development and rotated the IEs around different sites. Some people joined the IE group at a junior level, were promoted to a different group—say, running a manufacturing line—and then returned to run an IE group later.

Every quarter I traveled to all the sites and met with the factory managers and IEs. I also began cowriting, with the factory manager, each IE manager's annual performance review, because I could provide valuable feedback on the local IE manager's performance relative to peers around the globe. None of the factory managers disagreed. In fact, none ultimately disagreed with anything we did. It all made sense, they couldn't and didn't disagree with our objectives, and we had the full support of top management. In any case, the changes evolved slowly enough that local managers had ample opportunity to adjust and to speak up, if they wanted.

The reaction of the IEs to these changes was extremely positive. Having been pushed down to the bottom of the totem pole, they were now excited and energized to do what they'd been hired to do and have a career as well.

As a result, over two years we accomplished virtually everything we set out to do. People did begin to move from the factory to the IE group and back. We were able to reduce the cycle time for complex capacity scenario analyses from three weeks to three days and eliminate virtually all modeling and planning differences between factories.

The key was people—getting the right people and being clear about what was expected of them. We allowed them to do what they truly wanted to do and gave them the training, organizational support, and resources they needed to do good work. Most of all, they became genuine players in the system. We did change systems and processes, but we did it through the people who made the systems and processes work. As Don said—even in a high-tech environment, leaders lead people.

CHAPTER 12

Leadership Is Stewardship

Anonymous

I was director of sales and marketing for the remanufacturing division of General Industries in Europe, Africa, and the Middle East (EAME), selling products manufactured by four factories—one each in France, Poland, Germany, and England. All the plants focused on remanufacturing light-duty engine parts, mainly for big-brand OEM customers making farm and construction equipment.

Normally, I would have reported to a general manager, but that position was vacant at the time. So, for the moment, an operations manager and I were basically running EAME and reporting to a boss back in the United States.

Remanufacturing is a second-life solution. If the water pump on your tractor or backhoe is leaking, you have the option to buy either a remanufactured pump or a new one. The remanufactured pump is a high-value recycled product. To rebuild it, we take a worn-out or broken pump,

---

The identity of the storyteller, as well as those of companies, other people, and locations in the story, has been disguised. Any similarity to actual people or companies is coincidental.

save as much as we can of the original, machine what's left, and add material and new parts to produce something that will perform as good as new at a lower cost to the consumer.

The problem we faced was that we would probably have to close one of the plants. Over the previous ten years, the quality of original parts had gone up dramatically, and they no longer failed as frequently. If things are only failing half as often, then the need for remanufactured parts is half. Consequently, it had turned into a very tough market. Demand was down, prices were low, and there wasn't enough business to support all four plants. In fact, all of them as a group were losing money.

The assumption among my peer group and my boss was that we needed to close the English facility, which was located in Manchester. Of all four facilities, it was the prime candidate because it was leased instead of owned and would be easiest to shut down. Key Manchester customers could be supplied from excess capacity in the other three plants.

But I didn't feel good about closing it. Because of my previous work at General, I had gotten to know the four facilities well. In some respects the Manchester team was the best in their knowledge of the work and their work ethic. Closing the plant didn't feel like an appropriate reward for such a good team. Plus, the inconvenience for Manchester's customers would be great. For many of them, Manchester was their sole source for the parts it supplied. Before moving these customers to a new General Industries plant, they would have to approve and qualify it, and that might put our relationship with them at risk.

In a last-ditch effort to keep the Manchester plant open, our team built a plan to save it. We set a goal of saving $100,000 a month in expenses and adding $200,000 in contribution or variable margin. For twelve months, the people there worked very hard to cut costs and increase production volume and revenue. They met their cost-reduction target, but we failed to win any substantial new products for the factory, mainly because the demand wasn't there. By the end of the year, it was clear we weren't going to meet our objectives, which we had agreed would result in plant closure.

I wasn't particularly satisfied with that solution and still felt as if we hadn't done everything we could. Knowing that a lot of our employees had worked there for twenty to twenty-five years and were hoping to retire from General, I believed we needed to think about what else was possible.

As it turned out, I had a good relationship with the general manager at Capitol Manufacturing, a large international manufacturing conglomerate, who ran its global remanufacturing business. I met him in the airport in Dallas-Fort Worth. He was wearing a Capitol Reman jacket, so I introduced myself. After that, we'd gotten to know each other a little. In one of our discussions, I had told him about the great team we had in Manchester—knowing that with acquisitions, you don't always get a great team. I knew Capitol was investigating options for investment in Europe, and we both recognized how important a good team is to a successful remanufacturing business.

While we at General were in the throes of evaluating plant closure, a trade journal published a news bulletin that we were closing Manchester. Though the closure may have seemed inevitable, the bulletin predated our actual decision. Interestingly, when the GM at Capitol read the article, he called me while I was on vacation in Venice. His question was simple— would we consider selling the business?

He and I talked in principle, enough to establish that he was interested. But before I could discuss anything substantial, I had to clear it with my boss and his boss. That was where things got interesting.

For General Industries to sell a factory to Capitol Manufacturing was unheard of. Even talking to Capitol was taboo. There's a real sense of rivalry between the two firms that goes way back. We don't compete in many markets, but the two companies are both headquartered in Texas— Capitol in Dallas and General Industries in Houston. Even bringing up the possibility of a sale was a very, very big deal.

My first conversation with my boss was revealing. We'd already gone through the difficult process of deciding to close the Manchester plant and had justified it to his boss and his boss, all the way up the line. Now I was coming in and saying Capitol—Capitol Manufacturing!—might be interested.

The risk for me became apparent with that initial conversation, when my boss raised the obvious question of how those above us would react.

"If Capitol is interested, how can the Manchester plant be all that bad? If the right decision is for us to close this thing, then why would they want it? If they can make it work, why can't we?" My response was that they weren't remanufacturing parts for the same markets we were, so they weren't dealing with the declining market we were struggling with. And they were bringing their own customer—the Capitol dealer network.

That was the first issue. The second was, "Well, how does this help Capitol Manufacturing? How does this give them some advantage in the marketplace?" Fortunately, in the European market, we didn't compete strongly with them. They had a relatively weak presence in our market there, agriculture and construction equipment, but were very strong in the automotive market, which wasn't our market. So we could work through this because the Manchester plant wouldn't help them compete with us.

I managed to get my boss comfortable. Then we went to his boss, and I know he went to his boss, the president of a multibillion-dollar global group. It was very informal—"We're going to close this plant. We've got an opportunity to sell it to Capitol. Just so you know, we're talking to them"—but it still had to go that high up. Closing a facility was a big decision and something that we took very seriously, but our leadership left the decision to us.

For me there was yet another issue. I had hopes of being promoted to the then-empty general manager's position. Pursuing this deal could put that at risk because I would be seen as the guy doing the deal with Capitol Manufacturing. I was on the line. If something went wrong, I would be in the spotlight. It would have been easy not to talk to our rival and just close the plant like they wanted me to. No one would have faulted me for that. I knew that if I went down this path and something went wrong, people were certainly going to judge me, and there would be consequences.

I went ahead anyway because of the people. It had everything to do with the people. During the year I'd worked with that group, I'd built strong relationships and developed real respect for the team because of the constant sacrifices they made on behalf of the company. And I felt it was only appropriate for me to reciprocate.

It went back to sitting through Don's class and thinking about those lessons since then—that leadership is stewardship. You're not leading one hundred people or one thousand people for your own benefit. You're leading for theirs. This was a clear example, in my mind, of stewardship. So I didn't really think twice about the risks. I knew they were there. But I also knew that Capitol was probably the best remaining chance we had of saving the plant and that it was worth that risk for the two hundred people who potentially would keep their jobs.

Once we had permission, we quickly began the process of looking at a potential sale. People from Capitol came to Europe within a week, and we toured them through the Manchester facility. We were completely open with our workforce. The first time the Capitol people visited, we had an all-employee meeting and told them what we were doing and who was there, which is unusual in an acquisitions situation. Usually you remain quiet and secretive. We cautioned the Manchester people not to tell anyone. It was incredibly important, we said, that they respect this information and not talk about it. They didn't tell a soul. Neither side ever learned of anybody outside the Manchester circle who heard about the pending sale, including General Industries employees who visited that location regularly.

During the process, I remember a couple of remarkable events. The first was when Capitol decided it didn't want to lease the physical facility in Manchester because it wasn't a fit for their requirements. The fact that the facility was leased and not up to General's standards either was a key reason that Manchester had been the facility selected for closure in the first place. The Capitol people came to us on a Wednesday and said, "If there's no alternative location, then we're out." The Manchester team, particularly the manufacturing engineering manager and another manager, jumped through hoops. By Friday, they had identified a great facility, negotiated an unbelievable price, and had drafted a layout of what the equipment would look like in that facility. They put it in front of the Capitol people, and they were blown away.

We knew that the Capitol team had been working for months on a project to build a factory in Germany. We were also aware from early discussions that they were planning to present their plans to their corporate board at an upcoming meeting. In the course of three weeks, the

Manchester team had pulled off an unbelievable feat and assembled a strong enough alternative that the Capitol remanufacturing group went to its board of directors with the recommendation to go to Manchester.

To their surprise, the direction they got from their board was, "You shouldn't be doing this in western Europe, Germany, or England. You should be doing it in eastern Europe, because that's where the demand is going to come from." That feedback caught all parties by surprise. The sale fell through.

Within a few days, we went to Manchester to break the news to the employees that we had to close the plant there after all. We announced the time line for closing, which would occur over a period of ten months. We planned to relocate the production done at Manchester to General's other plants. The people at Manchester were deeply involved in the closure process.

We worked hard to help the people move on. We trained and coached them in resume writing and interviewing. We brought in job agencies and held a career fair to help them find new jobs. And we worked hard to place people at other General sites. There were three other General sites in the United Kingdom, but the closest was a fifty-five-minute drive. Unfortunately, 75 percent of the Manchester people didn't own a car. That was the key reason we were able to redeploy only 15 or 20 percent of the people—less than we'd hoped.

Early on, we published a redundancy schedule, dates when individuals would no longer be required, to help them make plans. In a number of instances, we pulled those dates forward or pushed them back to fit with individual circumstances.

In all these ways, we tried to demonstrate through our actions and not only our words that we truly cared for every individual in the process. It was the sense of stewardship that Don talked about. My staff and I, supported by my boss and his boss and the folks further up the chain, worked hard to save the business, then to sell it, and finally to help everyone through the transition as best we could. We took that stewardship very seriously.

As a result, the relationships, instead of being destroyed, grew deeper. People busted their humps right up to the end. They were genuinely appreciative of the efforts of my team to exhaust all alternatives to closure. They stayed focused on the work they had to do and didn't fall into the trap of nonproductive behavior.

One of the stories I clearly remember involved a machining center that was moving from England to France. Now, the English and French didn't always get along that well. The fellow in Manchester who programmed one of the machines recognized, given how the French planned to use the machine, that they would need about twenty new programs written. Nobody would have batted an eye if he had just left that work for the French to do. No one expected him to do it. But he took the initiative to write those twenty programs himself before the machine was crated up to ship—just days before he was laid off.

We worked hard to redeploy another fellow internally and actually made him two different job offers that he had to turn down for family reasons. As a salaried employee, he worked eighty hours his last week on the job, ineligible for overtime, tying up loose ends.

There were many stories like that. Everyone worked hard right up to the end, and many went way beyond what anyone would expect.

If I had had a chance to visit with Don about this experience, I don't think he would have seen it a whole lot different. He was passionate about doing the right thing. That was evident in the way he opened up to us in class in such a genuine and transparent way after a full and successful career as a CEO and in a setting where he didn't have to. He chose to do it. That was a powerful testament to what he believed—that you're a much more powerful leader, and you have a much more powerful influence on folks, if they can relate to you and feel that personal connection.

In the end, my team and I followed our gut and did what was right for these people. Leadership is stewardship.

CHAPTER 13

Learn to Say, "I Don't Know"

Heath Holtz

"**Y**ou want to go look on the floor?" said Jim, one of the managers reporting to me. I knew from the wary look on his face and his incredulous tone that this wasn't the response he'd expected. He had called me a short while before—I could hear a little panic in his voice—to report that one of his workers had been hurt on the job. I was new in my position, and it was my first OHSA reportable injury, something we took seriously.

When I arrived at Jim's office, he immediately rushed through an explanation before I could say or ask anything. He had already determined that the worker involved was personally at fault.

"Yes," I said, "I'd like you to show me what happened." He still looked confused. "I've worked in other plants," I said, "but never a car plant. I don't have any experience with this kind of injury. I need you to help me learn."

Still uncertain, he took me to the manufacturing floor, and together we walked through and analyzed what happened. Apparently, asking questions and reviewing an incident wasn't the approach taken by my predecessor, who responded to most problems by blaming the person in charge.

I headed the internal logistics department at one of the larger US plants of a global car maker. My group was responsible for taking material from the receiving door to the line. It sounds simple, but it required unpacking, picking, setting up for subassembly, and putting material in order—one of these, two of those, one of that—based on the sequence of vehicles coming down the line. Our goal was to get the right material to the right place on the line in time to keep production flowing.

It was not an easy start for me. Still learning the company, I was going into manufacturing in an unfamiliar plant after a year and a half in sales and marketing, where I had headed a small team of planners. Now I was responsible for a group of three hundred salaried and hourly employees and eight hundred contract workers.

My direct staff of six men and one woman ranged from forty to fifty-five years old. None was especially glad to see me. I was a thirty-year-old guy they didn't know much about. The two older men were indifferent. One was about to retire and had no interest in making any changes. The woman had been handpicked by my predecessor and had expected to get my job. She'd researched my background and questioned why I was there. That uneasy interaction with Jim, one of the younger men, was pretty typical in those early days when I was trying to learn the job and make some connection with the people I was supposed to lead.

When I arrived, we were already 20 percent over our labor and overhead budget. My immediate task was to get costs under control while maintaining the group's good safety and quality record. The team knew the operations but had not effectively managed costs. In fact, cost controls in all areas were inadequate. For example, until then it had been acceptable to manage head count without regard to the contract employees—temporaries who worked as needed.

The basic problem I faced was an old manufacturing management style, where the job was to do what the plant manager wanted. "I want you to build this new process" or "I need to add a quality check" or "I need you to put in this type of a pick area because we're struggling at the manufacturing line." Whatever the manager wanted he got without any cost analysis or business justification. So the department hadn't been run as a business. Instead, the work was just managing requests. Managing requests and, above all, not stopping the production line. That was the ultimate test. If you didn't shut the plant down, it didn't matter how much it cost. It was still success. Just do what you're told and keep the plant running.

But that didn't work anymore. When I walked in, the previous manager had just been told, "You're $8 million over budget. Do you realize that?" He had a limited understanding of where all the money was going. He didn't realize that it wasn't smart business just to blindly do the tasks in front of him or that it was his job to analyze, optimize, and then propose a better business solution to management.

Changing the mindset and culture of the place was a huge challenge because the previous manager had been old school in his management style. He had belittled the younger men on my staff, those in their mid-forties, in front of their hourly workers. So, they were afraid to make decisions. They seemed glad to have a different boss. Yet they were still leery because they didn't know me and wondered why someone so young had been put in charge.

Much of this was new to me. How do you change the culture of an organization so stuck in the way it does things? How do you manage out long-time employees, if you have to do that, or significantly reduce temporary labor staff? How do you lead teams that are much more experienced than you? As a young air force officer, I had led older enlisted personnel, but that was a common occurrence in the military. Here, promotion had always been based on experience and tenure, and all my people had more than I had.

I vividly remembered Don going through his mantras. I couldn't recite them all, but in my new position, one stood out for me: admit when you don't know something. I even remember his stern facial expressions in class and how adamant he was when he said, "Don't be afraid to admit your mistakes or when you don't know." He didn't do this in my class, but I've heard in other classes he would ask, "Can you say 'I don't know'? Let me hear you say it." And he'd make the whole class say out loud, "I don't know" and "I was wrong."

So, from the beginning of my new job, I clearly said, "I have internal logistics experience from my last company, but it's not the same here. So please explain this to me. I don't understand." Or, "I don't know this as well as you. Would you teach me?" At first suspicious, they soon realized I was sincere, and they welcomed my candor. This approach didn't compromise my authority because I still sometimes disagreed with them after I learned from them. It helped me gain credibility. When Jim and I walked through the injury and how it happened, for example, I ended up disagreeing with his assessment, based on my experience outside automotive manufacturing. But I said I understood his point of view and would support him in this situation based on his experience. In the future, though, I needed him to consider my point of view.

What I learned from Don wasn't just the ability to say, "I was wrong" or "I don't know." Behind that mantra, I always thought he was pushing us to be open, explore ideas and options, and demonstrate a desire to learn. So I listened a lot. I went from group to group and did introductions, and I conducted focus groups with hourly workers. Each week I met one-on-one with my managers and set up meetings every morning with them to review specifically what was going on. If there was an issue, like an accident or a downtime incident, we did a "go and see." We'd walk to the area and reenact what had happened.

I also made clear that I trusted their judgment. Before making any major decision or change, I'd look across the table and ask, "Does everybody agree? If you don't, now's the time." And I made clear what decisions they had the authority to make on their own, without my approval. I told them, "I will support your decision 100 percent—you're on my team." I also assured them that if I had an issue—if they ever decided something they should have checked with me first—I'd support them in public, and we'd talk about it in private. And I always tried to give them unfiltered feedback: "This is where you stand." I didn't want them surprised at a performance review or when someone else got promoted over them.

Most of them had been with the company for many years and were very good at what they did. They were relieved to have someone who was engaged and willing to listen and learn and who allowed them to do their jobs. Opening that door, letting them be who they were, was a big change they all welcomed.

It didn't happen right away. They had to learn they could trust me. In the beginning, some of them assumed I was just going to criticize and belittle them. But within a couple of months, once they realized that I really wanted to understand their work and that we would make changes as a team, I had the full support of five of the seven who worked for me. I was fortunate to report to a director who was not only blunt, but who had been at the plant for twenty-five years and knew these people personally. So I had unfiltered feedback from her. She would pull me aside and say, "They're all speaking highly of you. They're big supporters. They like your willingness to come in early and stay late to learn what's going on and that you're listening to them and letting them to do their jobs."

I could sense that they were getting more engaged in the work. As I gave them more freedom, they seemed to involve me more in matters they typically hadn't shared with their previous manager. They were inviting me to work with them.

Over the next year, we collaborated to develop an overall vision and mission for the department, along with some guiding principles and a process for making decisions. We created a strategy team that initiated numerous improvement and planning activities, and we began to make substantial change.

We did a deep dive into costs and operations and identified areas both to reduce and eliminate. The group had never focused on financial performance before. We made significant cost adjustments and developed an understanding of what was driving costs. Our work paid off. We reduced contract head count by 50 percent and got our monthly spending down to budget, while achieving record quality and all-time minimum downtime too.

Despite all this, the woman who had expected to get my job stayed at a distance. She only answered my direct questions and rarely volunteered anything. To spend more time with her—she was in charge of the night shift—I would come in very early and do a night-shift review with her. If there was a safety or downtime issue, I would arrive in the middle of the night and have her walk through it with me. That approach worked with the others, but it wasn't nearly as effective with her.

As I spent time with her, I was open about where I saw her strengths and weaknesses and how others perceived her and her performance. It took eighteen months for her to understand and accept the truth—that she hadn't been the next logical person and that she needed to prove herself. It took time for her to trust what I was saying.

She and I never developed the close working relationship I had with some of the others. But now she comes to me as a mentor—"Should I do this role?" Or "What do you think about this job?"

Looking back, the experience of owning up to what I didn't know and trusting and empowering others shaped my career, not as a single event or crossroad but as a series of learning points that you usually hear about only in leadership classes.

What I took away from Don's teachings was a sense that what I was doing as a leader was appropriate. He taught me that even a successful CEO can say, "I don't know." Prior to that, I'd thought that a second- or third-level manager or director had to know everything. Don reminded us that the higher you rise, the less you actually know about details. You should understand more about the business and have a larger vision than the people who work for you. But you may not know the specifics, so you have to trust people.

It's interesting that the mantra of the new head of manufacturing for the Americas at our company is "Be a Learner." Constantly ask questions. Always try to learn things outside your area. That concept aligns well with Don's teachings. Admit your mistakes; acknowledge when you don't know. The whole intent is to learn from your mistakes, seek insight and the expertise of others, and learn as much as possible about the organization and the diverse people who work there.

CHAPTER *14*

Followers Choose Leaders

Anonymous

After graduating from MIT, I went to work as an engineer, trying to improve yield for a global maker of high-tech components. Less than a year after I joined, the company launched a major new product line. When that happened, we saw a massive increase in demand and began shipping tremendous volumes of product. The plant where I worked had to expand much more quickly than anticipated and soon found itself short staffed in the production-manager area.

Over a two-week period, I received a double promotion—we called them "battlefield promotions"—and went from being a line supervisor to a production manager for about half the plant. The company desperately needed managers, and I had both line experience and a reputation for getting things done, plus I had the MIT pedigree—which opens doors, whether you deserve it or not—and my boss was one of the more powerful people in the plant. Suddenly, I found myself a second-line manager leading some four hundred to five hundred people.

The identity of the storyteller, as well as those of companies, other people, and locations in the story, has been disguised. Any similarity to actual people or companies is coincidental.

Introducing and ramping the plant to this new line of products, which had become the company's flagship line, was a key part of my responsibilities. The ramp rate was incredible and the technology still relatively immature. I'll never forget the day we spent throwing out all the inventory in the plant when the company found a design flaw in the product line. That only increased the pressure on us, which was enormous already, because we were shipping a large portion—eventually about half—of total corporate revenue through our plant.

In fact, though the ramp progressed in fits and starts, it was actually proceeding relatively well. Our plant and I were getting our fair share of accolades. All in all, in spite of the pressure, I felt good about the job we were doing.

One day, after I'd been in my new position about nine months to a year, my boss, John, pulled me into his office.

"What aspirations do you have for your career?" he wanted to know.

I said my current goal was to become a plant manager.

"Well, that's going to be tough to do, because all your people hate you."

I was taken aback. He was saying I was failing, in spite of the numbers. On the other hand, I wasn't completely surprised. I was sure people were complaining. I knew people weren't happy with the situation. I didn't think they were happy with me.

We were all spending horrendous hours—my wife will tell you it was the worst two years of our marriage because I was never home—and we pushed, pushed, pushed people. The culture in the plant at the time was very hard-charging—take no prisoners, get it done at all costs, in some cases by brute force if necessary.

My team was overworked, frustrated, and tired, and I was pushing them harder and harder to do more, at times beyond what they were comfortable doing. A couple of memories capture that time for me.

Working in the plant was both mentally demanding and physically draining, because the factory was perhaps four hundred to five hundred yards long, and you were constantly walking from one end to the other. It was probably common for someone to walk seven to ten miles in a day. We had break policies, but one day someone came to me, said the break policy wasn't adequate, and asked for additional time. I refused and basically said, "I don't understand. We have a break policy, and that's it. So-and-so can do it. We're not going to individualize the policy."

This was an eighty-five-pound Vietnamese woman. She had nowhere near the stride that others had, and the constant walking must have taken a toll on her. But I felt that the rest of the team was doing it and she should just suck it up. It was a callous response.

I'm a pretty laid-back manager, even-keeled, nonconfrontational, and noncombative, which are comments I hear sometimes in my reviews. But on one occasion back then, I remember yelling at somebody.

At a key step in the manufacturing process, the products had to undergo testing. If you don't get the settings right, you can actually destroy the products you're testing. For whatever reason, someone trashed $20,000 worth of product one day, and I basically laid into him in front of a bunch of people. Even at the time, I knew better—you know, praise in public, correct in private. Afterward, I felt really bad about that, and it's one of those things I've never repeated in my career since. It was immature, embarrassing, and unprofessional. I apologized to the person, but the damage was done.

I was also putting a lot of pressure on myself. I was hungry to climb the ranks and get to the next level of managing people—as fast as possible! I wanted to make an impact. I've talked to a number of MBA students since then, and they've generally shared the hopes and expectations of rapid success and career progression that I had back then. Why else would you take two years out of your life and what was probably already a successful career track, work like crazy, and, in many cases, incur a lot of debt if you didn't have high aspirations?

"Don't get me wrong," John said that day in his office. "You're hitting all the numbers. The plant is doing phenomenally well under the circumstances. But, that said, what you're doing isn't sustainable. Your team is going to mutiny. You can't drive people to a point where they break."

John had been running plants at the company for eons, and he had this sixth sense about everything going on. He could sit at his desk looking at all the monitors and just know when things were aberrant. I remember times he would call me on the plant floor, wanting to know, "What the hell is going on with the such-and-such machine?"

Of course, I had no idea, but when I checked, there would be a problem, and I'd think, *How could he tell that?* He had this uncanny mental model for how the plant worked. He was also a good guy with a big heart, though he could be pretty blunt and surly at times. He was a good mentor to me, and he genuinely cared about the plant and the people. So, I trusted him and paid attention to what he said.

"OK, John," I said that day in his office. "Walk me through this. What do you mean?"

"You don't care about your people. You probably view them as just the means to an end. Do you know them as individuals? Do you know what motivates each one of them? Do you know their hot buttons?"

I had to admit, at least to myself, that I didn't.

"If you look at the managers who've done well here," he said, "they're technically very competent, and that's a foregone conclusion. But they also have teams that want to follow them. I think you've got it backward. It's a pull, not a push model. You get people to actually do something by motivating them around a target and having that be the energy stimulus, not pushing people to do something."

That hit home. John was telling me in a not-so-subtle way what I'd heard in Don's classes but obviously hadn't understood or taken to heart. He was repeating one of Don's favorite mantras: "Leaders don't choose their followers. Followers choose their leaders."

When I was in Don's class, I saw in him a number of interesting qualities that I wanted to emulate. Here was a guy, the CEO of Stanley Tools, who, in retirement, chose to teach at MIT. Why would he do that? He certainly had other things going on. In fact, I had occasion to spend more than average time with him and was struck by how regular and down-to-earth he was. He changed my conception of a CEO as an unapproachable captain of industry. But I can't say his classroom mantras made an immediate impression. Obviously, given my approach as a manager in this job, I hadn't absorbed or even understood them.

Now I had a real-life boss, someone I respected, not only repeating what Don had said but telling me I was on my way to failure because, in effect, I hadn't taken Don's lesson seriously.

That conversation with John was only the beginning. First, I went and talked to my people. I still had good personal relationships with them, and it wasn't as though I couldn't talk to them. I asked them outright what they liked and didn't like about my management style and what I needed to change.

They were pretty open. "You're your own worst enemy," they said. "We know you're smart and you have a promising career, but listen to us. Stop telling, and flip around the quotient of listening to telling. We're happy to do the right things, but you have to listen, because you're not the smartest guy in the room. You're one of many. So shut up, listen, and get out of the way occasionally."

They also said it wasn't all about me and my success. "If we felt you cared about us more," they said, "we would do more to help you be successful. But right now we're doing the bare minimum just to get by. We're not passionate about coming to work because, through a combination of being coerced and burned out, we're not having fun. We're not putting our all into it because we just want to get through the day."

They were asking me to trust them, something I don't think I had been willing to do. I had to be the one calling the shots. In hindsight, John was right. I wasn't treating people like individuals but like the proverbial cogs in the wheel, pieces of equipment. They were only instruments to get the job done and get me to the next level. And so, all they heard from me was, "Do it. Get it done." To be honest, it *was* about me, me, me. I was hungry and aggressive, so I focused almost entirely on hitting the objectives at any cost and looking good in the process.

In hindsight, it was clear I didn't know what I was doing in management. I was in way over my head and not ready to admit it or ask for help. It was, in fact, a bad situation. Everybody was under the gun. The demands on all of us were enormous. But I was also to blame. I wasn't helping. I was increasing the entropy in the system, not decreasing the entropy. And until John pulled me aside and reminded me of what I already supposedly "knew," I was basically oblivious to my own management challenges.

I was lucky to have this painful experience early in my career. I consider it one of those formative moments that forged who I am today at work, because it was the impetus to change. Besides talking to my people and a number of conversations with John over several months, I went out and bought books about being a good manager, and I found good people who could serve as models and mentors.

You can't mechanically flick the switch and be a good leader. It was an evolution, a multiyear journey of, quite frankly, changing values in which everything stopped being entirely about me. That moment with John may look like a miraculous turnaround, but it was really the end of one chapter and the beginning of a longer story.

It was probably several months before my people would have said I had begun to change in significant ways. By the time I left two or three years later, I think people were having fun. I still hear today from people who worked for me then, or I run into them, and some of them even tell me, "You were one of the best managers I ever had."

I laugh and say, "Well, I started out as one of your worst managers. The fact that I ended up one of your best managers is a funny story in itself." I'm now a senior executive at another major high-tech firm, where I have some of the highest scores on the company's employee satisfaction survey.

As Don used to point out and I finally understood, leadership is all about having people actually want to follow you somewhere because they respect you, want to learn from you, and truly believe that you put their interests and career aspirations in front of your own. It's in essence treating people the way you want to be treated. I tell people that all the time. There's a very simple lens. If this were being done to you, would you like it? What would you think?

CHAPTER 15

Lead Up, Not Just Down

Anonymous

A few years ago, I went to Vancouver, Canada, to run a business unit that had just been acquired by Jameson Industries, a giant global industrial conglomerate.

We designed, purchased, manufactured, mounted, connected, and integrated customized equipment for the oil and gas industry. What we produced could range from relatively small units to large modular units that had to be disassembled and carried on multiple wide-load trucks to the customer site, where they would be reassembled.

Though the acquisition had closed only a few weeks earlier, I was astounded when I walked through the door at how much change had already been planned and was underway. This was a $20 million business with about sixty employees and sixty contractors, but from the very beginning, the chaos and complexity made it feel like a runaway train. Several people from my new boss's office in Toronto were coming and going—changing phones, e-mails, computers, and systems.

The identity of the storyteller, as well as those of companies, other people, and locations in the story, has been disguised. Any similarity to actual people or companies is coincidental.

From that chaos quickly emerged some serious issues. It was soon clear, for example, that there were no controls over procurement—how it was done, who did it, or who could sign a contract. Similarly, the estimates made in pricing potential projects for a customer were unreliable. We might sell a project in the millions of dollars without actually understanding what that project would cost us to deliver. We weren't sure how to measure labor on a project, nor could we determine who was responsible for defining each stage of the process from design through procure, build, test, and deliver.

These deficiencies were only made worse by the fact that my boss's team had already unplugged the company's legacy enterprise management system and replaced it with the SAP system Jameson used. The problem was that all legacy data was effectively unavailable—it had been archived without the ability to retrieve it easily—and the Jameson SAP system was not configured for managing the kind of large projects at the heart of our business. As a result, we were virtually blind. We had no way to understand the past, no way to make intelligent estimates for the future, and no useful way to track current operations. It certainly didn't help that a number of the company's more knowledgeable, experienced people had retired just before the acquisition.

On top of all this, I worked hard to understand the projections and estimates that had been used to justify the acquisition. What had been committed to Jameson in terms of what this business could deliver? How big could it grow? What would our profit margin be? I needed to know what I was expected to deliver.

As I learned the answers and began to understand the business, I realized that the commitments made to Jameson would be impossible to meet. For example, behind the vastly improved profit margins that the estimates projected was the simple assumption, unsupported by any analysis, that Jameson's superior knowledge of manufacturing would quickly cut our labor costs in half.

My first reaction was that I had to sit down with Richard, my boss, agree on new projections, and communicate those back up to the company. Unfortunately, that was more difficult to do than I expected.

Richard sat in Toronto, almost a continent away from where I worked in Vancouver. He reported to Roger, who was country manager for Canada, and Roger reported to Pierre, who was president of the Americas.

Prior to this position in Canada, I had managed another Jameson business unit in West Virginia. When I took that position, the unit was losing money and struggling with serious supply and pricing issues. Within eighteen months, we were able to correct the pricing and turn the company around with new product and marketing strategies.

In that job, I had regular contact with Pierre, who was one of the senior people monitoring and overseeing my success in West Virginia. As a result, he knew me and my work, and I think he had confidence in me. I certainly respected the guidance he'd given me at that time.

A second source of critical help at that time was Jack, then retired but formerly president of our Jameson division for the Americas. He happened to be living in the West Virginia town where my business unit was located, and he became not only a coach and mentor in everything from leadership to strategy and accounting but a friend whose advice I sought in many different situations.

I considered Pierre and Jack examples of the leadership Don Davis used to talk about, especially in his first and second mantras: "Leaders don't choose their followers—followers choose their leaders" and "Followers choose leaders they trust, respect, and are comfortable with." They were leaders because I chose them, and I chose them because I respected and looked up to them.

My new boss in Canada, Richard, didn't fit that mold, in my estimation. When I tried to work with him on the problems I'd identified, it became clear that his leadership style was not about discussion. He told you what to do, and that was what you had to do. We quickly began to butt heads.

He had been responsible for recommending the acquisition. He and his team in Toronto had done the analysis, including the assumption that labor costs could be cut in half. Naturally, he disagreed with my assessment that the projections were unrealistic.

That put me in a terrible bind. I felt my job and reputation were on the line. If I was going to say, "Yes, I can commit to delivering the plan that Richard created," I knew I would be accepting failure because I couldn't deliver.

Yet Richard was never willing to have a real discussion about the issue. We couldn't even have a decent meeting. He would come from Toronto, and, if the meeting was set to start at 8:00 a.m., he might show up at 9:00 a.m. He would keep his Blackberry on the whole time, and every time it rang, he'd say, "Sorry," and withdraw into another office.

When we did talk, he only wanted to discuss the SAP reports he was seeing in Toronto and how I was going to produce the numbers he wanted to see there. But because the system had been set up so poorly, you couldn't trust what it said. For example, most items we procured had to be put in the "Other" category because the system didn't have the classifications necessary to book them correctly against project plans. We also couldn't track labor costs accurately against specific projects.

It was a no-win situation. I was expected to produce unrealistic results with a system that couldn't be trusted and a boss who wouldn't discuss the problems. He was the hero who'd championed this acquisition that promised wonderful returns, and now he had someone running the company who was trying to tell him that the promises he'd made were terribly wrong.

The only solution I could see was to grow the company rapidly. If we stayed the size we were, we would lose money year after year, because we couldn't deliver the projected profit margin. We needed to go after larger projects and that, over time, through economies of scale, would enable us to grow and produce higher margins. Richard didn't accept this approach, because it would require more time and investment than he'd predicted. But it was the only way I could commit to something close to the original plans.

A few months after joining the company, we held one of our first business reviews, which Pierre as well as Richard attended. I used the opportunity to talk about my plans for growth. Pierre accepted and believed in that vision. In fact, he believed in it so much that he hired Jack, my previous coach and advisor, to help me put this growth plan together. That felt like progress to me. I had the approval and support of my boss's boss's boss, and I knew that Jack would be a supporter and a good coach for dealing with the problems that would come with the transition to this new approach.

Richard wasn't happy about my relationship with Pierre. During his visit for that business-review meeting, Pierre asked me on the spur of the moment to show him one of our units at our remote facility (about twenty minutes from our main facility). I did, but because it was last minute and completely unplanned, I didn't think to include Richard. Later, I learned that Richard felt I was undermining his authority by inviting Pierre to see the business facility without inviting him. In fact, Richard wrote me an e-mail full of directives, one of which said, "You will not talk to anybody above me or outside of your business unit without first informing me of what is to be communicated."

Richard seemed to feel he and I were in some sort of competition. Early in our working relationship, he asked me how old I'd been when I became a vice president at Jameson. I said I couldn't exactly remember, and he insisted that I figure it out. I did, and he said, "Oh, you beat me by two years." Somehow, that was important to him.

Richard's and my conflict was more than a disagreement about strategy. It came down to day-to-day conflict about how I should be spending my time. I wanted to focus on the steps that would produce greater growth. Richard wanted me to focus instead on hitting the projections he'd made in proposing the acquisition, which didn't assume the need for dramatic growth. So when we did meet and he concentrated on the dubious SAP numbers, he'd tell me to spend my time on things that I felt were taking attention away from long-term improvement for the company.

A prime example concerned change orders for projects that had closed before Jameson bought the company. In his acquisition analysis, Richard had claimed we would go back and collect for changes that various customers had ordered but hadn't paid for. In total, he said there was $1 million in profit from this source—not a small sum for an operation our size. But when we began talking to customers, it became clear the potential was at best a fraction of his estimate. I couldn't justify spending valuable time—my own or any of my key people's—chasing one-time, not-very-significant windfalls that wouldn't fix the business. There were too many other pressing issues with real long-term payoffs. His priority was producing the numbers he'd promised.

I remember thinking how Richard, unlike Pierre or Jack, illustrated the opposite of what Don talked about in his mantras. Someone at MIT once asked the question, "If your title were taken away, would people still follow you?" For me regarding Richard, the answer was certainly "No."

On the other hand, Jack, my coach and advisor, was a great help, and I relied on him. He pushed me hard—so hard I remember thinking at times, "I don't want to see you again." But every time that happened, I would sit back and think about it and realize he was right. He used logic and sound thinking, and he had my and the company's best interests in mind.

With Richard, I held my tongue and tried to be polite. I tried to make amends and fix things. But if you asked me who I actually followed, who was truly developing me and leading me in my role, it would have been Jack, because I trusted and respected him.

Jack had regular phone calls with Pierre and then would give me feedback. "Pierre likes what we're doing," he might say. Or, "Pierre believes in this strategy. It's the right plan. He's all over this growth. He wants you to put the capital request document together for top management." I was excited by having a business strategy that the top executives were interested in. Yet all the while, Richard and I couldn't agree on priorities.

I talked to Jack about this problem, and he didn't trust Richard either. So he often called Pierre and said, "Pierre, we've got a couple choices here. We can go this way or that way. Which way would you like us to go?" When Pierre answered, Jack would say, "OK, we also want to go that way, but we're not so sure that Richard and Roger are on board with that. Would you maybe have a chat with Roger and see if he can have a chat with Richard?" This approach worked well when something really critical had to be done. It would go from me to Jack to Pierre to Roger to Richard. Then, Richard would bring it back to me and say, "This needs to be done."

After several months in my new position, Richard sent me an e-mail with what I called "my orders." It was a numbered list of points that almost literally began by saying, "Let me tell you how we're going to work together. Number one: You will do what I tell you to do. Number two: Your controller will do what my controller tells him to do." Number three was the point I mentioned earlier: "You will not talk to anybody above me or outside of your business unit without first informing me of what is to be communicated." It went on like that for something like a dozen points.

I was so enraged that I immediately forwarded the e-mail to the Canadian VP of HR and asked him to drop by my office sometime that day, if he could. He was at my desk in fifteen minutes—he had been working at the company's regional office not far away—and the first thing he said was, "Please don't resign." He and I talked, and then I called Richard's office in Toronto to arrange a time for the two of us to talk.

To help me hold my tongue when he got on the phone, I even wrote out the points I wanted to make—something like: "We need to talk. We clearly don't understand each other. You must have misunderstood something I've been trying to do. I'm clearly not understanding what you're asking me to do. I can't work like this." I was going to suggest that he come to Vancouver and I would spend as much time as we needed to clear this up.

But when his secretary answered the phone and heard who it was, she said, "Richard said he can't speak with you for the next week. He'll call you the week after next, at his convenience."

Not long after that, Jack talked to Pierre about the problems Richard and I were having. Pierre went to Roger and said, "I don't know who's right and who's wrong, but I want the two of them to sit down and agree on a list of priorities for the next twelve months."

I wasn't happy that top management was getting involved and giving us a homework assignment. But if it forced Richard to sit down with me and agree on a set of priorities, that was good. I worked on my list pretty hard with help from Jack. I think it had four items on it, the items that I felt "if we can achieve these four things in the next year, that will be great."

We scheduled an all-day session in Vancouver to go through our two lists and produce an agreed-upon final list. But when the day came, Richard didn't show up until just before lunch and, as usual, left his cell phone on. His approach was basically, "All right, I've got my list, so why don't we go through my list and then we'll be done for the day." His list had about thirteen items on it—more a laundry list than a set of priorities. Only two of the items on my list happened to fall on his list. We spent maybe two or three hours talking. At one point he had his controller back in Toronto join us by phone to explain to me why his priorities were more important than mine.

I stuck to my priorities. At the end of the day, Richard basically said, "Well, let me think about it, and I'll come up with a final list, and that's what I'll send to Roger and Pierre."

I never did see the final list. The following week—this was late in June—Roger called me. "We want you to take the summer off," he said. "You can keep your computer. You can use your telephone. You'll still be paid. You don't need to use any vacation time. Toward the end of August, I'll call you and we'll figure out what your next role will be."

I was extremely disappointed and called Jack. He was floored. He called Pierre, who was upset because he had no idea this was going to happen. But he didn't undo it. He did call me to say he was very disappointed in the decision Canadian management had made, but he felt that some time off for me over the summer, if I could look at it in a positive light, would be a good thing. They would find something for me in the fall.

In the end, I left the company. Jameson actually came back and offered me three positions in other countries, one of which was a clear promotion. That pleased me. It felt like an acknowledgement that I hadn't been entirely in the wrong. But I had just gotten married, and my husband's professional career was tied to Vancouver. So I needed to stay in Canada, and the only positions available there were lower level than my previous job.

After all that happened, I thought about it a great deal. What we talked about in Don's class helped me see that, in hindsight, I might have done some things differently.

Don talked about not passing up an opportunity to exercise leadership, and that's what I did. I think it was my responsibility to lead up and not just down, to escalate important issues until they were resolved. In my frustration with Richard and his unleader-like behavior, I took no responsibility for our relationship when I could have done more.

I could have forced the discussion with him. I could have stood up more often for what I thought was right. I could have engaged earlier with

Roger, the head of Canada and Richard's boss, to help Richard and me have a better discussion. Perhaps I needed to be more proactive and go more often to Toronto. I wasn't relentless enough.

That was partly because having a focused discussion with Richard was difficult to do. Partly it was because I had the support of the leadership team reporting to me in Vancouver. But in large part it was also because I knew that Jack and Pierre supported what I was doing. So I thought it didn't matter that Richard and I disagreed.

That was a mistake. At the end of the day, I realized my approach didn't serve anybody well. As a leader, I needed to have Richard and Roger aligned and not just Jack and Pierre. I don't recall that Don ever talked explicitly about leading your boss, but in this situation that was a key part of leading the business unit I was responsible for. My relationship with Richard was an opportunity to lead that I didn't take.

Now, in a different role and a different industry, I'm applying what I learned. The first lesson is to seek out a boss you respect as a leader and can learn from, someone who will support your success and career growth. But for bosses who are less than ideal, seek out a coach or advisor who can help you find ways to understand their priorities and work with, not around, them. I'm fortunate today that my boss is someone I respect. I know I can't always pick the person I report to, and so I'm also, on the side, identifying coaches within my industry who could help if I find myself in another difficult setting where leading up is a critical part of my role.

CHAPTER *16*

If You Know Something's Wrong, Just Keep Talking

Anonymous

Several years ago, I became engineering manager for the US operations of Blaxton Products Co. (BPC), an international producer of machinery used in a wide variety of industrial processes such as manufacturing and refining. I reported to Bob Pierce, VP of operations for the United States, who reported to the president of Blaxton America.

The company had been founded more than forty years earlier by Alfred Blaxton, an engineer, when he created a line of innovative industrial mixers. For years a growing variety of mixers were the firm's only product, and they earned a reputation as being the top of the line. Mixers remained our signature line, but around 1990 Blaxton began to develop and acquire other lines of industrial products, so that by my time with BPC,

---

The identity of the storyteller, as well as those of companies, other people, and locations in the story, has been disguised. Any similarity to actual people or companies is coincidental.

sales were approaching $1 billion, and mixers were roughly only 35 percent of that.

Not long after my promotion, Al Blaxton "retired" to the chairman's position, and he brought in Roger Dome to replace him as CEO. Dome had been an executive with one of the global majors in the field of industrial products, the kind of company BPC aspired to become.

Literally within a month or so of joining, Dome pulled my boss, Bob, aside and told him we should be looking at outsourcing our manufacturing operation for mixers, which had always been produced in the United States. Dome apparently had led a very successful outsourcing effort at his previous company. "You really need to be moving in this direction," he said. "Why don't you figure out how we can do this?" Bob handed off the assignment to me as the head of engineering.

It made me uneasy. When it came to mixers, BPC was best known for its build-to-order sales model and eight-day fulfillment. Virtually from the beginning, the company had distinguished itself by the high degree of customization it allowed the buyers. In fact, we had become so good at it that our prices usually rivaled those of our competitors, who were producing to stock, and we had equal or better margins. Our manufacturing was done at three US plants, where our longtime workers had deep experience in our heavily IT-driven manufacturing processes.

When Bob first passed on the assignment, my reaction was, "Boy, no one else in the world knows how to do this. If we're going to outsource this, we'll literally have to teach outsourcers how to do it. How can we prevent them from selling that to our competitors?" Bob didn't disagree, but he also knew that Roger had given him more than a simple suggestion. It was a marching order.

I was curious though. "Does Al"—that's what everyone called Mr. Blaxton—"know about this? Does he think it's a good idea?"

Bob said he'd asked that question, and Dome had assured him that Blaxton was "100 percent on board, full steam ahead."

"All right," I said. "Let me analyze it, pull together an RFQ, and figure it out."

I pulled together a team of six or seven fairly senior people, and the first path we went down was getting estimates for outsourcing the whole operation, soup to nuts, to a third party. For that we approached all the outsourcers who were known in the industry and doing it for our competitors.

That took a while, in fact, a lot longer than I think anyone expected. Whenever someone pressed us, I always explained that we were taking extra care to put out robust RFQs. We wanted the most accurate estimates we could get, and we wanted to make sure outsourcers knew exactly what went into the kind of build-to-order manufacturing we were doing. Our process front to back looked 100 percent different from anyone else's. We didn't want them sugarcoating the numbers they came back with. We carefully analyzed everything they sent us, and we even met with many of them to make sure we understood what they were giving us and they understood exactly what we needed.

The outcome was clear. There was no business case for outsourcing. Without charging uncompetitive prices, we couldn't justify manufacturing our customized mixers, say, in China and then airfreighting them to the customer, but that's what was required to meet our eight-day commitment.

Our competitors, like Dome's old company, could outsource because they were manufacturing in bulk based on a specification and shipping finished product back on a cargo ship, which significantly reduced the logistics costs. We studied that too. We tried to figure out which of our customers might be willing to wait sixty to ninety days. It turned out to be only a small subset, even for a price break. So, we couldn't make the analysis work for outsourcing the whole operation. When you analyzed everything, the fixed and variable costs and the savings from good inventory management, there was really no argument for going down that path.

When we presented Dome with all the data and analysis we'd done and showed all the costs and risks and that it clearly didn't make sense, he got mad and said, "You didn't do this right. I'm sure these guys can figure out how to do it cheaper. Go back and figure it out. There must be at least some processes we can outsource."

He even tried to pick apart our analysis. Inventory costs, for example. We had correctly assumed higher costs there, because outsourcing would require higher inventory levels. He said the outsourcers would bear those costs. We wouldn't buy the finished goods from the outsourcers until they got to our shore. When I pointed out the cost of inventory was a cost the outsourcer would have to cover, he just said, "Ah, you're overthinking it. I'm telling you this will work." His experience at his old company convinced him it could be done, even though our manufacturing approach was completely different.

After that meeting, we went back and did a detailed mapping of all our manufacturing processes and looked for ways we could save money by outsourcing some of them. We did find some candidates, and so we looked at those in detail. That was a huge effort, since it meant the outsourcers had to be even closer to our current manufacturing because their work would have to lead into and out of our work. We literally looked at putting up buildings for the outsourcers on our sites and connecting them to our buildings by conveyors. In the end, this was a wash, but only with very creative accounting. For example, this approach had high fixed costs—all those buildings we had to put up—and the numbers for that worked only if we took credit for the space in our own buildings that was freed up—while ignoring the fact there was no other use for that space.

We also looked at having outsourcers staff our production lines in our US plants. The outsourcer could save some money there by paying lower wages and benefits than we normally paid. But they had to make a margin, and so, again, at the end of the day, that approach was a wash at best.

Every week or two, I met with Bob, my boss, and Tom Lancey, the VP of finance, who was also deeply involved from the accounting side. I don't know how much of this was coming from the CEO through the CFO, but Lancey really wanted to make outsourcing work. And so he was putting a lot of pressure on me. For Bob, though, it was more complicated, I think. He was too professional to say so outright, but he was a real manufacturing guy like me, and I think he didn't buy into the idea of outsourcing for our build-to-order operation. His boss, the president of the Americas, was basically a sales guy, and he seemed happy to pass on any pressure from the CEO. Bob was caught in the middle. He had to meet periodically with Dome to update him, and I gather those meetings were just awful. The whole thing was a political nightmare for him.

In my regular updates with Bob and Tom Lancey, I would pass on the latest numbers from our analysis, and they hated them. It was not the message they wanted to hear, because all this pressure was rolling downhill onto them to do it. And so the two of them would argue with me. Sometimes the arguments spilled over into other meetings. It wasn't unprofessional. This was a big topic for debate, as you can imagine, that affected every one of Bob's direct reports, my peers. I was the most junior person on Bob's staff at the time, and every person pulled me aside at least once and said, "You need to think about this." It affected everybody. It was debated at off sites and at staff meetings.

I definitely pushed the edge of the envelope in arguing with others, including many leaders senior to me, about what kind of sense this really made. In spite of all the pressure, I just refused to move things along quickly and did every last bit of analysis to make sure that when we presented it, we really knew what we were talking about.

To be honest, if I had thought outsourcing was the right thing to do, I'm sure we would have gotten through the analysis a lot quicker. I remember thinking back at the time to Don's class and what he had told us: "If you know something's wrong, just keep dragging your feet." That was the approach I took. In my heart, I knew this was wrong. Quite honestly, emotionally, my career had been dedicated at that point to manufacturing, and I was passionate about it. But I was genuinely worried too. There was real danger here for the company. If we had gone ahead quickly, the way everyone was pushing us to do, we would have had an outsourcer just give us a number. Outsourcers wanted this business, and so we easily could have gotten ourselves into a contract the outsourcer ultimately couldn't fulfill. But then, once you've fired all your people, you're stuck. It was a one-way street. Once you did it, there was no turning back. Delay avoided that and gave us enough time to pull together the analysis with all the real facts.

I know Dome was frustrated. He knew I was leading the team working on this, and, even though I was three levels below him, he used to buttonhole me in the hall and want to know what was taking so long. "This is obvious," he'd say. "You just need to make it happen."

And I would always say, "Well, we have a team working on it, and we're pulling together the numbers."

Then he'd go beat up on my boss, Bob, who would tell me, "Stop arguing with the CEO. You're killing me." I guess I was supposed to be afraid of the CEO, but I really wasn't. Being junior in this situation was almost an advantage, because I didn't have the same career fears that more senior people had.

After many months we finally finished and made a preliminary presentation to Dome. My boss was under incredible pressure. If we'd gone in and made a presentation against outsourcing, Dome probably would have had him fired. So we pitched it as a wash based on some very creative accounting and on not highlighting the risks but not hiding them either. Dome liked it and told us to prepare a full presentation for Al Blaxton.

I was too junior to be at that meeting, but I put the presentation together for Bob to present. He practiced it three or four times with me and others on his team in the two weeks leading up to the presentation. That was all stressful, a lot of debates. I was adamant that he present it as accurately as possible. I wanted to make sure it did justice to all the work we'd done and didn't hide key facts that made this look like a bad decision. The night before the presentation, I wrote Bob a four- or five-page e-mail about how I believed this was wrong, the reasoning behind it was wrong, and it would be the wrong legacy for him to leave. I don't think either of us slept that night. I sent my email around 3:00 a.m., and he replied around 5:00 a.m.

In the end, I think Bob was a genius in the way he finally pitched the analysis. He believed that Al Blaxton was ready to outsource, and so he pitched it as a kind of gut check—here are the pros and cons, here's the financial data, here are the possible negatives. There's no guarantee we'll save money, and maybe we'll lose money, but because we think it will be about the same cost, we're recommending it. He could have spun the data to make it look more positive, but he didn't. He made clear it wasn't a no-brainer, but we were recommending it because it was the "right strategic move," the way the whole industry was going.

I wasn't there, but I heard what happened. It was company practice to open every presentation with a summary slide that laid out the key information and presented the conclusion. Then the remaining slides presented all the backup. For this meeting, that first slide laid out the pros and cons and financial metrics and then said, "Because this is the right long-term strategy, we recommend outsourcing."

The meeting apparently never got past that first slide. Once Al understood what it was saying, he asked, "Why are you even looking at this? We would *never* consider outsourcing this." The meeting was scheduled to take an hour and a half or even two hours, but it was over in less than thirty minutes. Obviously, Dome had misunderstood or misrepresented Blaxton's willingness to consider outsourcing.

As soon as the meeting broke up, Bob contacted everyone and told us the outcome. Then, that week, he took the whole team, including spouses, out to dinner. He knew people had killed themselves working nights and weekends on the analysis, under pressure, and he understood the frustration. Then, at the end of the dinner, it was back to business. He told everyone, "You're still accountable for all the cost savings in our original plan for this year, and now we're at least six months behind." He was reminding us that analyzing outsourcing options hadn't been the way we'd planned to spend the first half of the year.

I never found out for sure exactly what was said by whom during and after that meeting. But I do know that, within two weeks, Roger Dome was literally moved out of the corporate headquarters building and into a temporary office near the bathrooms in a different building, and that he left the company probably ninety days after that.

Sometimes I wonder if all that analysis and foot-dragging I did really made a difference. Would Al Blaxton have killed the idea no matter what we presented? Maybe. But I still think that if we'd done what we were supposed to do—go create some numbers that made outsourcing the obvious choice—he might have felt compelled to go along with his new CEO who'd had so much success at his previous company. I believe Don's advice was right in this case. It was a situation in which the quick answer was, "Yes, go ahead," but the long answer, the right one, was not to outsource.

Even after all the analysis I insisted we do, we did end up delivering cost savings for the year far superior to our original plan. We had an incredible year after that, in fact, and probably got two years of work done in six months from an engineering and a process engineering point of view.

CHAPTER *17*

Leaders Set the Tone for the Organization

Anonymous

Several years after completing the LGO program, I took a position as the operations manager in a division of Zentec Inc., a $250 million industrial equipment maker and a subsidiary of Argen Industries, a global Fortune 200 corporation. I had full operating responsibility with a staff of people to support me in running four manufacturing plants, three in St. Louis and another just outside the city.

It was exciting to be entering a field of manufacturing that was new to me. Plus, my division, previously a privately held company, had been recently acquired and was still going through something of a turnaround under Zentec's wing. I looked forward to being part of that.

This change was also a new life for my wife, five children, and ailing in-laws who moved to St. Louis to stay close to us. It took a while,

---

The identity of the storyteller, as well as those of companies, other people, and locations in the story, has been disguised. Any similarity to actual people or companies is coincidental.

but finally we had everyone placed in new schools and senior-living facilities as I settled into the job.

Unfortunately, in spite of my initial excitement, something seemed amiss about the company and the work almost literally from the day I walked in the door and began to see how the place operated. That feeling came initially from the fact that the eight-person management team I joined consisted of a close-knit core of five who had worked together for years.

As general manager, Sam headed the division. He had been promoted from the position I now held when the former general manager had been promoted to a position at Zentec headquarters in Providence. Apparently, the two of them were still close. The three new people in the group included, besides me, an HR manager and a customer service manager, both of whom had moved to the division from other parts of Zentec in the previous two years. The remaining four included two engineering managers (product and manufacturing), a sales manager, and a quality manager. They and Sam had worked together for years. In fact, most of them had never worked anywhere else.

When I was interviewing for the job, I'd been told by Sam and the Zentec corporate staff in Providence that I would be the number-two person in the division. That's why I took the job. I was even shown Sam's old office, right next to his new office, where I would sit. I was glad for that. As the number two, it was important for me to have a strong, ongoing working relationship with my boss.

But when I showed up my first day, one of the engineers was using the office I'd been told would be mine, and I was shown to my office, the engineer's old office, which was out in an island on the plant floor, completely away from everyone else in the leadership team.

This is strange, I thought. But, being the new guy, I didn't want to make a big deal of it. I was flexible. Still, it made me wonder what was going on. To deal with my boss and the others, I would have to walk through the plant and into the administrative office area, and that was a physical barrier between them and me. It would take away the spontaneous conversation and problem solving that happens when people work next to each other.

There were other things too, like lunches. Typically, when you first join an organization, people reach out and say, "Hey, let's go get some coffee," or "We're heading out to lunch, would you like to join us?" None of that happened here. That group of five all stuck very close to each other. There were even times when I happened to be around as they went out for lunch, and they'd walk right by me and never invite me along.

Over time, it also became obvious to me that this group would resist any effort to change things. On many occasions, I went to Sam and said something like, "Hey Sam, I really need your help. I'm having difficulty getting support from Herman (the manufacturing engineer) on such-and-such initiative in one of the plants."

Sam would say he'd think about it. Then, he and Herman would talk without me, and the next thing I knew, Sam was coming back to me saying, "Hey, I talked to Herman, and I don't think we should do what you're suggesting. Let's just leave it the way it is." There was a lot of that.

Those five were like family members who let each other get away with anything. There was no accountability or pressure to improve. For example, the sales manager was a single woman in her sixties on the tail end of her career. She'd worked there before and openly said that she came back to St. Louis to "take care of her folks." As sales manager, she'd travelled all over the world on Zentec's dime and never secured a deal. She never came back with substantial business to justify being in Europe for three or four weeks every other month. There was no accountability, no pressure on her to book orders or do business.

Another example was the Tiger Level One program, a huge quality initiative that came all the way from Argen corporate, which was pushing it in every company it owned. It was the Argen equivalent of one of the Toyota production systems. It established criteria that said, "Thou shalt solicit market feedback analysis from all your major customers. You need to do side pocks, supplier input pocks, and customer mapping for all your major processes. You need to have X number of people proficient in the Tiger operating system. You have to conduct X number of value-stream mapping activities; X number of kaizen events, etc., etc."

Shortly after I joined, Sam sat me down and explained that we were pursuing Tiger Level One, the highest level of certification, and our goal was to become Zentec's first Tiger One facility in North America. For Sam, who had just been promoted into a general management role, it would give him lots of visibility and cement his and the former GM's transformation of this division from a privately held company to a leading member of the Zentec group. Tiger Level One was a big deal.

I wanted to be deeply involved, and so, after I'd been there two or three months, I went to Sam with a suggestion. I was unimpressed with the professionalism of June, the quality manager who was managing all our Tiger efforts. "Would you consider having June report to me?" I asked. "When you sat in my chair, she reported to you. Since I'm responsible for all plant operations, it would put me in a better position to influence what we're doing in preparation for Tiger Level One." Sam said no. He had to admit it made some sense, because she used to report to my position when he was in it, but he didn't want to make any changes now. He said he wanted to stay close to the program.

It was frustrating. There I was, several months into my job, trying to get a feel for the lay of the land and the people I could trust. Who could I go to when I needed help fixing a problem? Who could I have an open, honest conversation with about critical things important to the future of the business? Instead of finding anyone like that, I slowly discovered this interwoven cultural fabric that excluded any outsiders and blocked any change. This core group of people had worked together so long—Zentec didn't move people around much to keep management teams fresh—that they did what they wanted and didn't seem to answer to anyone else.

All that was bad enough, but I slowly realized it was even worse.

After a while, I began to notice that Sam often came in late. There were times I went into his office midmorning and sat across the desk from him and could smell alcohol. In my previous position, there was a fair amount of drinking among hourly employees, and we were trained to recognize when someone was under the influence. I got good at it. Over time, I had many mornings with Sam when I'd think, *He's drunk.*

I never confronted him about it. How do you do that with your boss? But it was clear what was going on. He'd come in drunk midmorning, but everyone around him kept their mouths shut. They kept it hush-hush because, in return, Sam would let them do whatever they wanted.

I also began to realize that Sam and June were both communicating information to Zentec corporate in Providence that was almost lies. A lot of the metrics they sent weren't anywhere near accurate; for example, on-time shipping performance. To qualify for Tiger Level One, you have to have at least 98 percent on-time delivery. I knew our on-time delivery was nowhere near that level, but June was scrubbing the shipping data to say that our on-time delivery was in excess of 98 percent.

The amount of fabrication became clear when we started to prepare for our Tiger preaudit. This was when auditors came in from Zentec corporate to look at all our Tiger data. Their purpose was to determine if we were ready to be certified by the official auditors from Argen. It was a preaudit to the official audit.

One of the key things auditors looked for was relentless root-cause analysis. Whenever there was a quality issue, we were supposed to investigate the problem, identify a root cause, put in a permanent preventive action, and then ensure that the problem didn't reoccur. It was called a "dive," which stood for define, investigate, verify, and eliminate. The auditors would choose specific problems and ask us to show them the dive done for each.

One day I was in Sam's office going through preparations for the preaudit. "We don't have a lot of dive reports for the entire last year," I told him. "They just don't exist." A majority of the dives that should have been done had never been conducted.

"You don't need to worry about that," Sam said. "That's something I'm going to handle with the audit team when they come in."

I really began to feel something wasn't right when Sam told me he was pulling every supervisor and salaried employee off the plant floors for two weeks. I pushed back on that. "How is it possible," I asked him, "to run four plants by myself with no salaried staff supporting me?"

He looked me right in the eye and said, "It's your job to get the people into this room"—we were sitting in a conference room—"so I can do what I need to do to prepare for Tiger One." I did what he said, and we managed to get by in the plants.

I wasn't invited to those working sessions. I wasn't part of preparing for the audits. And I wasn't officially supposed to know what was going on. But all those people in the room worked for me, and they eventually told me what they were doing. Sam led the meetings every day and literally had them fabricate over seventy dives over the past two years so that when the audit teams came and asked about a particular problem, they could immediately bring up the dive that had been done. Only it hadn't been done when it was supposed to be done. It was "done" three weeks prior in that meeting room.

I was uncomfortable with that obviously. Don Davis had said, "Only you can lose your integrity," but it wasn't clear what I should do. It was my boss, the general manager of the division, who was leading the whole thing. I could have called the ombudsman, but it was standard practice when something went to the ombudsman for him to notify the general manager of what was communicated.

Since this was an internal company matter, I decided my approach would be to work with the preauditors when they came in. When they arrived, I singled out the most seasoned veteran among them, who had been doing this for years it turned out, and who knew all the senior leadership in Zentec, because he'd grown up in the organization with them. I paired up with him as he went through and performed his assessments. Without blatantly accusing my boss of flagrant dishonesty, and while trying to reinforce areas where the company had made a good-faith effort to abide by the Tiger criteria, I also made sure he understood where there might be a lack of substance in the data. He was very smart and intuitive and probably had seen every trick in the book. He figured out what was going on.

Off-line he told me, "None of these facilities are perfect, and one of the overarching purposes of the program is to pull them along." Instead of focusing on what might have been fabricated, he chose to focus on the positives coming out of the attention being placed on trying to make things better. He was forthright with me. "This is something that I personally deal with as I go from facility to facility," he said, "because we, as auditors, get phone calls from senior leaders in Providence that usually go like this: 'Hi, nice to talk with you. I hear you're going to do a Tiger assessment at one of my facilities. Boy, I'm really happy that you're going to do that Tiger assessment at one of my facilities. We're really looking forward to becoming Tiger certified. Ha ha ha.'"

He also told me that the Tiger results go all the way up the company chain of command, not just Zentec but Argen too. "We can't go back to Providence and tell the corporate team we're not moving forward with Tiger certification," he said. "The senior Zentec leaders with responsibility for this division all have goals and bonuses tied to having X number of Tiger certifications by the end of the fiscal year. It would even get down to the Argen team in Wilmington." There were multiple levels of politics involved. "You definitely don't want to be the guy who steps in front of this train," he said.

I heard what he was telling me, but I was still concerned about what had been done. It wasn't a minor oversight or rounding some number up a tenth of a digit. Sam and June took every supervisor and manager off the plant floor, put them in a conference room, and had them spend two weeks making up data. To me that was really, really egregious.

So when the official auditors came in to do the actual certification, I took the same approach. This group included someone from Zentec corporate. I spoke with him one-on-one many times, and he picked up on the phony data almost from day one. His feedback to me was exactly the same as I had received from the fellow who did the preaudit. "You think as an assessor I can come in and block the certification," he said, "but this goes way up into the corporate hierarchy, and it is what it is. It's not that they're breaking the law. There's no criminal action here."

He was right. There was nothing illegal going on. And no one's safety or health was being put at risk. But it wasn't good. It was the cultural fabric of the organization that was being broken. What did making all my managers and supervisors part of a huge scam tell them about being honest in their daily work in the plants?

I didn't like it, but figuring out what to do about it was hard. I made sure both sets of auditors knew what was going on. I assumed they'd seen this kind of situation before and would know what to do. Apparently, they'd learned that the right response was to do nothing. I never directly confronted Sam with what he was doing. He was going to do what he was going to do. I think it would have been insubordination if I outright accused him of falsifying something. If I did that, there was a good chance I'd be fired. Both auditors had made clear—and they had deep experience in both Zentec and Argen—that in their estimation no one at company or corporate headquarters wanted to know the details of what was being done.

I can't say what I did or didn't do was right. Don talked about "doing the right thing" and said it was usually clear what that was. It didn't feel that clear to me in this situation. At this point, I began to think my only option might be to find another position, much as I hated the idea of uprooting my family again and working through all the turmoil a job change involves.

An event that followed shortly after the audits helped me decide.

Every year the division held a strategic off-site to step back and do some planning. This year it was going to be at a resort in the Ozarks instead of, as usual, at a local hotel. Sam's whole leadership team was going, and the plan was to arrive and socialize on Thursday evening, spend the next day on planning and team-building exercises (Sam hired a firm out of Chicago to lead this), socialize again that night, and drive home Saturday morning.

We carpooled to the resort in three or four cars Friday afternoon. Sam had rented a set of condos there, plus a condo that we all used as a meeting and social center. We knew Sam had arrived early to set up, but we all wondered where June was, because she hadn't hitched a ride in any of the cars. We all checked in, settled into our own condos, and then went over to the social center—to discover June there with Sam. That seemed slightly strange; apparently, she had travelled with Sam. But no one said anything.

After socializing a bit, we all went to a nearby steak house and had a nice dinner. Then we went back for more socializing, maybe some cards or other games. Pretty soon, everyone noticed that Sam was pounding down one beer after another—to the point that some of us worried he might pass out. Others were drinking too, and after a while, one or two others and I decided to leave. We had to meet at 7:00 a.m. the next morning for breakfast and the first workshop.

Friday morning several of us showed up per the schedule and realized that some people weren't there, including June, Herman, one of the engineering managers, and Sam. When someone asked about it, the people who'd stayed late the previous night started to chuckle. They said Sam had gotten ripping drunk and stayed up until 3:00 a.m. They apparently had seen Sam on the bed with June during the evening.

We went ahead with the morning schedule—mostly it was a big team-building scavenger hunt—without Sam and the others. When we returned to the social center around noon, they still weren't there. Finally, around 1:00 p.m., they straggled in, eyes bloodshot.

The people from the outside firm took us through the rest of the sessions planned for the day. That evening, after dinner, was supposed to be more socializing, but I didn't feel comfortable staying for another night of the same. Jerry, the customer service manager—like me, he wasn't part of the inner group—felt the same way, and we decided to drive home together that evening. He had stayed longer than I had at the previous evening's socializing and hadn't been amused by what he'd seen.

With these people, in these circumstances, leaving early felt like a big decision. I would be saying I wasn't part of the group and didn't want to participate in what they were doing. It was a message to Sam that I wasn't going to play ball. It was the first time in my professional life that I had to make a decision that could potentially slice my throat and my career.

I went to Sam and told him I was leaving. I'd been there for the actual business sessions, and now I wanted to get back to my family for the weekend. "No problem," he said. "Go ahead." But I could sense the unsaid words between us as to why I was leaving and the impact it would have on our relationship. I believed, as Don used to tell us, that what we did as leaders set the tone for the organization. It wasn't a good thing for leaders to get sloppy drunk to the point where they puke or pass out on the floor or give the impression, regardless of what actually happened, that something was going on between them and people who worked for them.

On the ride back with Jerry, we decided that word of what had gone on needed to get back to company headquarters. Since Jerry was the division ombudsman and had extensive contacts in Providence, we decided he would make the call.

Not long after the off-site, we learned that the division had been certified Tiger Level One, and Sam was getting congratulatory calls from company vice presidents. I'm sure it helped that the senior leader in Providence who was our Tiger sponsor was apparently the most organizationally astute and plugged-in Tiger representative there.

About a month after that, all the management staff were called into a special meeting by Ken, Sam's boss and the former general manager in St. Louis, who'd flown in from Providence.

"I'm here to let you know," Ken told us, "that effective this morning, Sam has been placed on indefinite administrative leave pending further investigation. I don't anticipate that he will be returning."

People from company HR conducted an investigation and interviewed everyone who'd been at the off-site, especially those who stayed for the second night, when apparently things had gotten even more rowdy. I was glad I had left, because it removed a possible cloud from over my head.

As Ken said, Sam did not return. Besides what he'd done at the off-site, I understand, he had also been submitting bogus expense reports for things like trips to Asia with June.

Sam's position remained open for a few months while the company looked for a replacement. One of the engineering managers and I filled in, and both of us were candidates to replace him. In the end, the company hired a new GM, Jack, from another Zentec company. I knew him slightly. He had a great reputation for being absolutely straightforward and ethical. The idea, Ken told me, was that, with Jack's background in sales and my experience in operations, we would make a good team.

But I had already decided that there was no future for me there. Even with Sam gone, the culture was so inbred and nasty that I knew it was unlikely to ever change or embrace me, the guy who'd refused to play ball. As Don often said, followers choose their leaders, and that group wasn't going to choose me, no matter what the company did.

After the off-site, I'd begun looking, and, by coincidence, I submitted my two-week notice the day Jack was announced as the new GM. He took me out to dinner and tried to talk me out of leaving. I said no because I genuinely thought he needed to start with a clean slate. My presence would be a hindrance to him, not a help.

I stayed in touch with Jack and a few others after I left. Eventually, he left too. He said he'd found what I had found—an old guard that had no desire to change and that made life miserable for anyone who didn't comply with what they wanted to do. That was one of the lessons I learned. It's very difficult, no matter how good you are, to come into a business that's been run by the same folks for decades, because you're dealing with someone's baby. These people have put their entire professional careers into the business. Any change you recommend, no matter how diplomatic you are, is likely to be an insult to their entire life's work.

That certainly doesn't absolve me of any responsibility for the way things turned out. I don't profess that I was successful in my role at Zentec. There were some gross oversights on my part.

A big one was related to Don's mantra about trusting your gut. An experience like mine quickly teaches you that your gut can be a wonderful compass. When something about an organization gives you that funny feeling that things don't seem right, usually it's because something really isn't right.

A big signal in this case came even before I joined Zentec. I still remember playing the phone message that said, "This is Henry Taylor calling from Zentec. We'd like to bring you in for an on-site interview."

I called back and set up a date, and when I showed up for the interview, I said to the guard at the reception desk, "I'm here to see Henry Taylor," and the guard said, "I'm Henry Taylor." *Really?* I thought. How many companies have hourly security guards doing HR work for senior positions?

I ignored my gut and didn't pursue the matter. I went on to have a great interview with Sam, who said all the right things then and in subsequent phone conversations about my role and how I would be the number-two guy.

I should have asked about it. After joining the company, I learned that Sam didn't get along with his HR manager, and so he would have Henry, the nine-dollar-an-hour guard, do many of his HR jobs, including the processing of expense reports that ultimately got him fired.

As a result of this whole experience, I've changed my approach. Since Zentec, I've had interviews for a number of different positions in different organizations, and I never hesitate to ask questions about culture or anything else that seems off or odd. I'm much less concerned about destroying my candidacy with hard questions, because I learned that, if my gut is sending a signal, I probably don't want to be in that environment, no matter how lucrative or prestigious the position.

CHAPTER 18

Don't Take Yourself Too Seriously

Anonymous

A fter graduating from LGO, I returned to Boeing and, following some interim assignments, became program manager for one of its military aircraft programs with a foreign government. The contract called for modernizing the mission electronics and installing a new radar system in this country's fleet of military aircraft.

I had been in this position less than six months when it came time for our annual award-fee determination. Under our cost-plus contract, Boeing was paid all allowed expenses, up to a set limit, plus an additional fee for profit. That fee could vary from nothing to 100 percent of the amount allowed, based on our performance as assessed by our direct customer, the US Air Force officer in charge of the contract. (The Department of Defense managed this kind of work, as prescribed by the Arms Export Control Act. Since this program involved aircraft, our contract was through the US Air Force.)

The identity of the storyteller, as well as those of companies, other people, and locations in the story, has been disguised. Any similarity to actual people or companies is coincidental.

Naturally, our goal was to achieve 100 percent or close to it. As the time for the award drew near, I heard many veteran program managers talk about Boeing's stellar performance over many years on all these contracts. We almost always scored 90 to 100 percent.

The letter announcing our award finally arrived, and I was summoned to my boss's office. Our score was a devastating 50 percent. It didn't matter that my seat had been in the program manager's chair only a few months. This was now my program, and the fee was my fee. In my position, I was responsible for Boeing's performance, including profit and loss, and our score meant millions of dollars in lost profit for the year.

As I searched the letter for reasons, it quickly became evident that our customer had based our dismal score on the performance of another contractor. Our contract, which was still in phase one, called for development of technical upgrades for several key electronics systems. In this phase, Boeing was responsible for all upgrades *except* radar. That fell to the maker of the radar system and was being done under a contract separate from ours. In the second contract phase—production—Boeing would be in charge of installing all upgrades, and the radar maker would be a subcontractor to us. Until that second phase, however, both we and the radar maker reported separately to the Air Force Systems Program Office (SPO) for these programs. I knew problems with the radar upgrades were delaying completion of this phase, but I hadn't been concerned because radar wasn't yet our responsibility.

When I saw our dismal score and the reason for it, my immediate thought was to get on the phone with the customer and say, "What are you doing? This isn't right! Radar isn't part of our contract! You can't assess us based on the performance of another contractor working under a separate contract." I was ready to go to war. It was just wrong. It was almost insulting.

My team had done excellent work over the past year in meeting the difficult technical challenges of retrofitting new systems into old aircraft. This shouldn't be how they and the company were rewarded. It wasn't just millions in lost profits. Pride and morale were involved too, not to mention that this would be a key measure of my own performance as program manager.

The formal way to proceed would have been to talk to our contracts management people and write an official letter challenging the award and explaining why it was inappropriate. I knew award-fee challenges virtually never led to higher fees, but I was convinced that we could win this case because it was black and white. The air force had no right to score us against standards not in our contract. This was an affront to Boeing, my team, and to me. I just couldn't let it pass.

As I was fuming, I remembered something Don Davis said. Someone in class once asked him what he considered the keys to his success. Part of his answer, one of the mottos he mentioned, was, "Don't take yourself too seriously." That really stuck in my mind. It wasn't something I expected to hear from a person who'd been a successful CEO for twenty years. Until then I probably thought the head of a major company would be tough, a stickler for doing things the right way, someone who didn't take stuff from anyone. But here was a successful CEO saying he didn't need to take himself so seriously all the time. He was telling us that, even if you're running a big company, you can back off at times and say, "Well, maybe I'm not right about everything. Maybe I sometimes need to step back and play something in a different way."

"Don't take yourself too seriously" might have held different meanings for different people. But for me it meant I could laugh at myself and accept a little humility. You don't always have to let your ego dictate how you behave. I liked that idea and realized it might be the right way to react to this situation.

Seeking vindication through a formal appeal wouldn't get us anywhere. It would only create animosity and make my customer and his boss defensive and mad. Taking my case public would reflect badly on them. I would be saying their score was unfair and unjust and implying that what they'd done was even bordering on the unethical. This might be a situation where I needed to back off a little, swallow my pride for a minute, and let them come to the right conclusion themselves.

Perhaps, I thought, *if I sat in a room and talked with my customer, the SPO officer, and his boss, that more personal approach might be a better way to understand the score they gave us and why they thought the other contractor should be part of it.* I talked to my boss, who ran all these programs for Boeing, and he concurred.

First, I had to convince my customer that a meeting was even necessary. The military was a very formal organization, and he could have simply said the score was final—end of discussion. Besides, I knew he was young and managing his first major contract, and he was trying to make a mark. Part of making a mark was to be tough and not let the contractor push you around. I'd seen some of that behavior from him before, though overall I thought we had a good relationship.

It was important that we meet sooner rather than later. Once he started to tell people the score he'd given us, it would be hard for him to back off. That he was new and out to prove himself would only make him less likely to rethink anything.

I called him and explained that I wanted to hear more about the rationale for the score. I wanted to understand all the reasons, good and bad, so that I could take them back to my team and improve our performance. That was true, though it certainly wasn't the approach I initially wanted to take. I thought a conversation about our performance would also give us an opportunity to talk about the other contractor and the scoring criteria he had used.

Fortunately, he agreed to meet, so I flew back to meet him in Virginia. I was more than a little bit anxious, not knowing how this was going to go. For me, the stakes were pretty high, and I knew there was little precedent for the customer to actually change an award.

When I walked into his office, I was relieved to see it was just him and his boss, as I'd requested. If he'd included anyone else—a contracts officer, say—it would have been too formal and hard to break down any barriers of defensiveness.

Though it was only the three of us, I could still sense some of those barriers when we began. Whatever reasons I'd given in asking for the meeting, they knew I was there to question what they'd done. So, with Don's motto in mind, I worked hard to be relaxed and make clear that I was there to understand their thinking, to hear anything negative they had to say, and not to challenge and confront them.

We walked through the elements of the score we received, item by item, and I was able to ask clarifying questions. When we got to the part of our score that reflected—unfairly, but I didn't press the point—the performance of the other contractor, we stepped away from the award fee specifically and just talked about the radar maker and the problems it was having. I wanted to know, for example, what specifically was causing the delays in its work.

As we explored those issues, I began to offer suggestions for ways the Boeing team could help the radar company improve its performance. Boeing didn't have that company's expertise in radar, but it did have deep experience in program and systems management. Even though we weren't responsible, perhaps there were ways we could help.

I could sense the air force people starting to soften a little and become more open to different ideas. When I suggested that my boss and I could help manage the radar maker, that idea was well received. At no additional cost, I said, we could go out, meet regularly with the radar company, and use Boeing's management skills to help them get through this development phase successfully. I hadn't talked this over with my boss, but it was certainly in our interests to help if that would get us all to the production phase of the contract sooner.

It gradually became clear as we talked that the 50 percent award fee had been a way of sending us a message. The customer was saying, in effect, "Well, Boeing, this is what we're going to do if you don't manage them in the next phase of this contract. You should have stepped up to do it now, because you know you'll have to do it later."

I didn't argue. There was no point in letting my anger drive my behavior, because it wouldn't help. All I could do was point out facts, and the key fact was that the radar maker almost certainly wouldn't have appreciated or accepted Boeing's efforts to manage it, since it was operating under its own contract. Though the customer thought we *should* have stepped up, he and his boss had to agree.

That was how the meeting ended. As I recall, we never talked specifically about changing the 50 percent award fee. I hoped our willingness to help the radar maker, with the customer's blessing, might make a difference. For all I knew, it might only affect the remaining, final award fee on the development contract, not the current award. The customer made no promises and only said he'd think about it.

I had to go back and tell my boss that I had offered to do more work at no additional cost and with no commitment from the customer to do anything about the award fee. It was a long week of waiting to see what he would do.

In the end, he did the right thing. He gave us 90 percent. As I read his letter announcing the new fee, I had one brief twinge of disappointment that it wasn't even higher, but then I remembered where we'd started. His letter provided no comment or explanation. He changed the fee, modified some of the other comments, and simply removed the part about the performance of the radar contractor. What was most interesting was that he revised our fee without our having asked for it officially. Normally, the only way to get a revision was through a formal request.

I don't know what might have happened if I'd acted on my initial reactions and gone to war. Raising a huge fuss might have made me feel better, but I think we came out better with the approach Don's words seemed to suggest.

CHAPTER *19*

Your Best Style Is Your Own Style

Rachel Sheinbein

I n 2010 I became president of the board of a highly successful nonprofit, Expanding Your Horizons (EYH), which conducts yearly conferences for girls curious about careers in STEM—science, technology, engineering, and math.

Run almost entirely by volunteers—women pursuing STEM careers themselves—the day-long conferences give young women, who are mostly in the sixth to ninth grades, hands-on experience with subjects ranging from evolutionary biology to computer programming to engine mechanics, as well as an opportunity to see and hear women already in STEM careers. Most conferences are held at a university, and so for many attendees, it is their first visit to a campus.

Founded in 1976, EYH runs more than eighty conferences each year for about twenty-five thousand attendees. Throughout its history, it has touched over eight hundred thousand young women. It is a gateway for girls to learn more about STEM, and surveys taken at the end of each conference show that these girls become more knowledgeable about STEM careers and more willing to consider one for themselves.

After six years on the EYH board prior to my new role, I knew the organization well. But, in spite of its obvious success and my profound belief in its work, I also believed EYH could do more to pursue its basic purpose and that, in fact, it needed to do more if it wanted to survive and thrive for another three decades and beyond.

However, compelling organizational and personal reasons made me think twice about pursuing that belief as president. When I thought about what to do, the lessons I had learned in Don's class at MIT provided important guidance. For several years, I'd kept my notebook from his class in my bedside table, and during this period I consulted it often.

I joined the EYH board in 2004, as its youngest member, because of my deep belief in the importance of women in STEM roles. In high school I had attended an EYH-like conference at a local university, and I vividly remembered the kidney dialysis machine we studied and an egg-drop experiment that demonstrated gravity and tension forces. That conference was an important early step in my ultimate decision to go on and earn an undergraduate engineering degree with a math minor, a master's degree in engineering, and an MBA.

As a student, I was well aware that STEM was not a typical path for women, but I thought it was important for women to enter those fields. As a chemical engineering major in college, I began to realize that technological innovation is the future of society. If we don't have women in STEM roles, we'll lose the ideas, talents, and diverse viewpoints of half our population, limiting society's potential for improvement, as well as its ability to consider the efficacy of new drugs, medical devices, and other innovations for both men and women.

From its beginning, EYH had followed a very successful grassroots, decentralized model that succeeded because of the passion of the local volunteers running it, who received minimal guidance or help from the national organization. In the late 1990s, a small professional staff came on board—a national conference coordinator who became executive director, along with a part-time office manager. Its primary goal was to get grants and keep supporting conferences.

Those who had been involved from the beginning felt justifiable pride in what they had accomplished. In another decade, they would be able to say they'd touched the lives of a million young women. The organization had clearly surpassed their hopes and expectations.

Yet there was frustration too. I would hear people say, "This organization is having such a big impact. Why doesn't it command the attention it deserves?" All of us had gone to gatherings of women in STEM and discovered that many there had attended one of our conferences or knew about EYH or knew someone who had attended. Why weren't we brought in on grants? Why were others starting new programs from scratch instead of taking advantage of what EYH had built?

Another problem was money. At my first board meeting, I discovered the organization was completely out of cash, and I watched one of the board members write a check to pay the executive director. I thought, *Wait. Don't we have a foundation or some other kind of support? If we got a dollar from half the alums who had gone through a conference, we would double our budget.* We were fussing over grants of $5,000 or $10,000 and felt lucky to get them. No one was saying, "We're doing incredible work. Organizations should want to be associated with the impact EYH is having." It didn't add up.

So, as president, I began to imagine the possibilities. It's my nature to always look for ways to improve any situation I'm in. I'm always asking, "What are the possibilities? Why not...? What else can we do?" The potential at EYH seemed enormous to me. We had a platform from which we could do far more to bring women into the STEM pipeline and help them persevere.

But it wasn't just a matter of finding and pursuing new opportunities. We were operating in a field that valued fresh ideas and growing impact. Yet EYH was doing exactly what it had done for almost three and a half decades. I saw other nonprofits start up and raise significant backing because they were new and exciting. Yet we struggled every year just to raise modest funding from corporate donors because we were doing what we'd always done for thirty years. If we wanted to attract attention and additional funding, we had to expand beyond our base.

Still, I hesitated.

Shortly after I became president of the board in 2010, the National Science Board gave EYH an award for its contribution to public education. I flew to Washington, DC, and spoke to 250 people at the State

Department. The award recognized the great good the organization had done and was doing. It brought to mind the old adage, "If it's not broken, don't try to fix it." If I pushed and began the process of change and it didn't work out, could EYH simply return to what it had been? Perhaps not.

I had other reservations. To create real change, I would need to bring along my colleagues on the EYH board, including founders and other highly accomplished women who were understandably proud of what they'd done and might resist putting it at risk.

I also understood that the course I advocated meant EYH would need more staff and infrastructure, and that meant we would have to commit to raising significantly more money every year. If we struggled to raise modest sums, could we change donors' perceptions of EYH enough to bring in considerably more money?

I had personal qualms as well. My work as a partner in a Bay Area venture firm was demanding, and I didn't know if I had the time to press for and see through significant change. I worried that I would instigate a process of change and then, once it was underway and irreversible, be overwhelmed by the time and effort it demanded of me.

As I wrestled with these issues and questions, I thought of Don, whose teachings had already played an important role in my work and career choices. EYH felt like the kind of leadership opportunity and need that he'd encouraged us to pursue.

One of the key lessons I took from his class was the importance of being authentic, the need for a leader to pursue his or her own instincts about what needed to be done. "Your best style," I remember he said, "is your own style." I've thought about that a lot. What he taught about authenticity resonated deeply with me, and as I gained more experience and confidence, the authenticity he encouraged was coming out more and more in what I did. Here, I realized, it appeared in my desire to make something good, something deeply important to me, even better. It was my need to press beyond the status quo. Being authentic and true to what I considered important meant taking on this challenge, even though it would have been easier and safer to stay with the status quo.

I'd never heard the idea of authenticity before Don's class. Only with experience did I grow to understand what he meant—especially that being true to yourself was sometimes hard. You could go through your entire career hiding from challenges and letting people tell you what to do. Or you could be true to who you really were and to your passions, and, if you were true, then you'd serve your company or whatever you were doing in the world better.

Those insights, especially about authenticity, gave me the courage to move ahead with the opportunities at EYH. One moment in particular stood out. I had been president for a while and was still absorbing Don's lessons and wondering whether to push the organization to a new level. Someone asked me, "What's holding the organization back? Why are you on a small budget and struggling to raise money? With all the impact you've had, what's holding you back?"

I paused for a minute and said, "You know what, we're holding ourselves back!"

I enlisted the support of other board members, and we're now building the staff and organization capable of moving to the next level in the ways I described. We just hired a new, highly qualified CEO who will spearhead the effort. My three-year term as president ended a few months ago, but the board asked me to stay one more year to provide consistency and support the new leadership as it comes on board.

Moving ahead was the right thing to do. As Don said, follow your own sense of what needs to be done, and don't let an opportunity to lead pass by. Although the EYH story is still in the making, I feel empowered by the changes I've implemented and grateful for Don's wisdom and inspiration.

CHAPTER *20*

Selfship Is the Enemy of Leadership

Stephen Cook

I joined Dell in 1998 and moved to Nashville in 2004 to manage a company plant that made desktop computers. At the time, it was the largest Dell plant and the largest company campus outside headquarters in Austin.

Over my first year or two there, I was able to put in place a team of high-potential senior managers who were doing a good job running the plant, and we were seeing real progress in moving toward our goals. I was dead set that this plant was going to be the best Dell plant on every metric you could measure.

One day in the spring of 2006, as I neared my second anniversary in Nashville, I was in my office on a conference call with the head of HR for the Americas. A call came in on my personal cell phone, which rarely rang, and so I excused myself and picked up. It was Connie, one of our children's teachers and a family friend.

"Steve, I'm freaking out. Alexis and Christian are fine," she said. They were two of my three children. "But a tornado almost hit the school.

There's damage everywhere. And I think it went through your neighborhood and hit your house."

"Connie," I said, "I have no idea what you're talking about. I'm sure a tornado didn't hit my house. Don't worry about it."

My family and I had just returned from a beach vacation the day before and hadn't slowed down enough to check the news. We hadn't heard anything about tornadoes.

"I can't get hold of Shannon," Connie said. Shannon was my wife, and I knew she was home with our four-year-old.

"Shannon's cell phone is a one-way communication device," I said. "She hardly ever answers it."

I wasn't worried. Growing up in the Northeast, I'd only seen tornadoes in television news reports, and, based on what I'd seen, tornados only damaged small-frame houses and trailer parks. I was sure people would be safe in the kind of big, sturdy brick house where we lived.

Back in the meeting, I told the head of HR, "I just had the weirdest phone call," and explained what I'd been told.

"Steve," he said, "you really should go home."

"No, no way. Let's keep working."

"No, you really should go home."

"I'm sure it's nothing. Let's just get through this meeting."

"You're not listening to me. I'm giving you an order. Go home."

He was a VP, and I was a director, so I said, "OK."

I left the meeting and started walking toward the elevator when I remembered that my aunt and uncle were flying in from New York that day. They were coming from the airport to the plant, where I planned to give them a plant tour, and then they would follow me to our house. They were due to arrive in about an hour, and I knew what would happen: I'd go home and find nothing wrong, while they showed up at the plant and I'd be gone. It was going to be a wild goose chase. So I convinced myself to stay and wait for them.

I hated to waste time. As a leader, I pushed people extremely hard, and I got great results. I pushed myself too. Since arriving in Nashville, I'd probably worked an average of seventy or eighty hours a week.

After less than a year in my new position, I had quickly become famous for something I said when we were planning my first Christmas party at the plant. The season between Thanksgiving and Christmas was the busiest time of year in our consumer desktop business. I was determined to keep the plant running no matter what, and I said, "Can't we find people who aren't going to the Christmas party and run the plant that night anyway?"

We worked every single day that year between Thanksgiving and Christmas, including Christmas Eve. All employees worked at least ten-hour shifts every day for almost thirty days without a day off. They had no holiday season. Exhausted after long days on the floor, they couldn't go Christmas shopping, wrap presents, or put up a tree with their family. I was completely focused on the customers—and on the executives above me who were giving me pressure. I was taking that pressure and amplifying it down on my team, which, you can imagine, was pushing back on me. "We've got to do this," I insisted. "We don't have a choice. This is what the business calls for."

Now, over a year later, as I paced the hall and waited for my aunt and uncle to show up, my personal cell phone buzzed—I had voice mail, which was odd because it hadn't rung. It was my wife.

"Jackson and I are alive, but we have no earthly possessions," her message said. "Get home as quick as you can."

To reach our house, I had to drive north and into the trail of destruction left by the tornado as it had travelled west to east. There was so much debris and so many delays, a trip that normally took twenty minutes took three and a half hours. I reached my neighborhood about 6:00 p.m., but the National Guard wouldn't let me pass until I convinced them I was going to get in one way or the other. They weren't allowing cars in at that point, but they let me run through people's lawns.

The tornado had literally come within a second or two of taking my wife and Jackson, our four-year-old. He had been outside when the tornado was ripping apart our neighbor's house. My wife, who'd thought he was in the bedroom watching a movie, grabbed him from the front door.

The wind was so strong she couldn't close the door. She was trying to shove it closed with her shoulder when the windows on both sides of the door shattered. She thought for a second the shards were hail. She gave up on the door, picked up Jackson, and started running in her bare feet. A ten-foot-tall picture window above the door came crashing down right behind them. As she sprinted through the house, all the other windows blew in. Thank God our house was one of the few in the neighborhood with a storm shelter—until then, we'd thought it was a complete waste of money. Running downstairs—the house sat on the side of a hill—she saw furniture flying by the window and finally realized, "Oh my God, I'm in the middle of a tornado!" She got to the storm shelter and managed to shut the door. Miraculously, her bare feet had survived running through cut glass.

Inside she listened to the house crashing down around them, with Jackson crying, "I don't like this, Mommy. I don't like this, Mommy."

"I don't like it either," she told him.

Our two older children made it to the house from school. Late that night, we finally got to sleep in the house of a neighbor five doors away, who was away on a temporary assignment. The neighborhood had no heat or electricity, and the night was really cold. That's how tornadoes work. You go from hot to cold, and that extreme temperature difference is what causes them. I had no idea of that beforehand.

The next morning was Saturday. After maybe five hours sleep and nothing to eat since noon Friday, I went back to what was left of our house. An F4 tornado had passed directly through it. The roof was gone, and so was the whole back of the house. It was like a movie set with a front and two sides but destruction everywhere else. It was only 7:00 or 7:30 a.m., but about thirty people from Dell were already there. They had rented two trucks on their own, and inventory control had let them take a large supply of boxes and packing tape. They were searching through the wreckage for anything worth saving.

Around 9:00 a.m., a group of Cub Scouts came by with homemade peanut-butter-and-jelly sandwiches. It was the best-tasting food I've ever had in my life. A little later the Red Cross arrived, and we began taking our meals from a Red Cross truck. It was the first time any of us had ever been on the receiving end of community service.

All morning, as Dell people sifted through the debris, they'd come to me with piles of stuff in their hands, asking what to do with it. One came to me with this pile of old notebooks from a closet that had escaped much damage. They were my notebooks from MIT. I grabbed the pile and began thumbing through them. The one I opened first happened to have material from Don's class, including the mantras, which I reread that day for the first time in the eight years since I graduated.

In the coming days and weeks, we focused on putting our lives back together. But finding my notebooks from Don's class and rereading his mantras, in combination with the tragedy we'd barely escaped, led me to rethink my work and how I'd been doing it.

First, from a personal point of view, I had been working more and more hours and getting further and further out of whack in my work-life balance. I hadn't even noticed that was happening.

Second, the mantras and the enormous support we received from Dell people led me to think about the kind of boss I'd been. On my long, desperate drive home the day of the tornado, I received many calls from Dell people, asking how they could help. This was followed by my surprise at finding so many Dell people at my house Saturday morning, pitching in to help. I was surprised because, honestly, I hadn't given them many reasons to be that loyal to me. Yet there they were, giving up a weekend, the whole management team, the whole HR team.

I thought of that when I read Don's mantra that leaders need a base of power and authority, but the more they use it, the less there is left. I likened it to a bank account. With all relationships, you're either making deposits or you're making withdrawals. As an awful leader, I was close to getting notices from the bank that I was bouncing checks.

In fact, I'd already received notices from direct reports, but I hadn't been paying attention. Some of them had pulled me aside and said, "You haven't built relationships with people, and you're just driving them like slaves. You're a good guy, but nobody knows that. You haven't built relationships." Also, Dell did 360 reviews, and my entire organization had told me that, as one of my former bosses would have said, I was getting results, but I was leaving some bodies—not in a horrible, negative way, but my account was definitely overdrawn.

The mantra that really hit home was the one that said, "Leadership is stewardship. Selfship is the enemy of leadership." I had entirely forgotten this one. I suppose I justified to myself that I was doing community service, which I had done all my life and which was now expected of me in my role. But it had always been a check-the-box effort, something I was supposed to do and not sincere. If I'd been honest with myself, I'd have had to admit that this service and my work had been all about me and my career.

The whole experience regrounded me. Finding the mantras and re-reading them was an epiphany. I had drifted away from them, and these events pulled me back in a huge way. I changed from viewing myself as a leader at the top of the pyramid to realizing that I was really at the bottom. I probably talked a good game about leadership before that, but I don't think I really believed it. I became focused on doing whatever it took to pay back this team for getting me and my family through this time.

I changed how I viewed my team as a leader, and it changed the whole dynamic of the plant. I spent more time on the floor and less time in my team room. Up to that point, for example, I'd allowed myself to be pulled into lots of phone calls. From a career point of view, that was probably a smart thing, but it wasn't the best way to lead my team or the plant. Now people would hug me on the floor, and I would hug them back. Or I would walk up and give them a hug. That was not me before at all. I'd come out of flying military jets, and, like the character in the movie *Top Gun*, I was "Ice." I was successful, and so people wanted to be around me. And people wanted to report to me because I had a good track record of taking care of my people. But I was not very approachable. After this experience, I became much more willing to share my faith with people. Not in an outward, pushing-it-on-people way, but in appropriate settings I would talk about how blessed I was and how passionate I was to take care of people. It was sincere and that came through, and it created a genuine sense of two-way loyalty.

The next Christmas my whole mentality shifted, compared with the previous year when I'd pushed people to work ten- and twelve-hour shifts for thirty days straight. Instead of pushing to do whatever it took to crush the metrics, instead of passing on and amplifying the pressure

I was getting from my bosses, I pushed back. "We're not going to do that. It's not humane. If the customer's shipment is delayed by one day, we're still meeting all the metrics. It's not going to miss being under the Christmas tree." We got every possible order out by Christmas Eve. No matter what, that had to happen. My first two Christmas holidays in Nashville, I had taken the pressure on me and pushed it downward. But the next Christmas, I took the pressure on me from my own team to take better care of our people and pushed it upward. As a thank-you, we gave a turkey to every employee. Though not necessarily a big thing, nothing like that had ever been done before. It was a sign of appreciation for everyone's hard work.

The next summer, a year after the tornado, I convinced the leadership team to do something else we'd never done before. In August, right after the end of our second quarter, we paid for every employee and up to three guests each to spend a day at Six Flags, a huge family amusement park nearby. For many of these people, it was like a family vacation they'd never taken before. After that, we did it every year on a Friday or Monday and negotiated a deal with the park that let people, if they wanted, spend the full weekend there for not much more money.

In the past, I wouldn't have done anything like that because I'd think, *This is going to cost the company a fortune, and it's going to hit my cost per box.* Now, I'd think, *This is the right thing to do. We're going to find a way to absorb that cost somewhere else, and we'll be more productive.*

About a year after the tornado, it became clear that Dell would need to close one of its plants. The market had begun shifting away from desktops, and that's what we and two other Dell plants made, including one just recently opened.

I was determined that we wouldn't be the plant the company closed. We went through a dramatic lean conversion. "We're not going down without a fight" was our rallying cry, and with a lot of help from our engineering group, we ended up twice as productive as the new plant, which Dell had spent $250 million building with high automation. We had better quality, and our cost per box was significantly lower than that of the other two Dell plants. So, the company decided to shut down the plant in Austin, the mother ship, the pride of Dell, the facility the company showed off to customers. We won because we wouldn't give up, no matter what. We were Dell's oldest plant, the one with the least investment, completely written off. And there we were, twice as productive as the brand-new, highly automated plant. It was like the United States beating Russia in Olympics hockey back in 1980.

I left my position in Nashville in early 2008. It was very emotional. I cried, and a lot of people, even on the floor, were hugging me and crying on my last day. I'd left positions before and nobody had cried, but this was different.

I left believing the plant was safe, since the Austin plant had closed. But shortly after I left, the company decided to outsource all manufacturing. No plant would survive. Fortunately, we had earlier convinced senior leadership to move Dell's refurbishment business from Austin to Nashville because we were more centrally located. Based on lower shipping costs for that operation if it were in Nashville, we were able to put together a convincing business case. That business remained in Nashville. It employed some five hundred people, not the 2,400 we had before, but five hundred was better than zero. Dell eventually sold that business, but it remained there with the same building and people, just a different name on the outside. It's literally the only plant from that time that still has an ongoing operation with employees. Saving the plant was a massive victory due in large part to the passion of the people and leadership team there.

Even to this day, I remain deeply loyal to that group of people. We have reunions. I've helped at least ten or fifteen of them find outside jobs when they decided to leave Dell, and I've helped many of them find promotional opportunities inside the company.

Three times in my life something has happened that I would have said beforehand, "That's the worst thing that could possibly happen." But afterward I discovered that they were key turning points in my life. The tornado was one of those times. It completely changed me as a person and a leader. It regrounded me, and it refocused me on my family and on what was really important to me spiritually.

For the first time in my life, I truly felt leadership was stewardship. I was asked recently by an investor, "Why do you love manufacturing?" The private equity fund where I now work focuses on manufacturing.

My answer was that "manufacturing is the only work I've found where I can combine my passion outside work with my passion inside work." When you're running a manufacturing plant, if you do a good job, you're taking care of many people who are one paycheck away from being homeless or on welfare. When you're running an engineering group or a private equity firm, none of those people are likely to be out on the street. When you run a large manufacturing operation, if you do your job well, you can positively impact hundreds and even thousands of lives.

After the tornado, that was how I viewed my role as a leader, and that was definitely not what I'd believed previously. Finding those tattered notebooks and reading back through the mantras crystalized my thinking. I had drifted from what Don had taught us. Perhaps, until then, I had never truly understood it. Now I get it, and he was absolutely right.

CHAPTER 21

You Can Be Successful and Still Have Balance in Your Life

Brian Feller

My most lasting memory of Don isn't from any one particular lesson or even one of his famous mantras. Even though I attended the class and, as Don's teaching assistant, helped him prepare and conduct it, I learned as much from Don the person as I did from Don the professor/ business leader.

I was one of the few students who had children. We had two, ages three and five, and one day I mentioned to Don that we were planning a camping trip to Martha's Vineyard, a scenic island off the coast of Massachusetts, about an hour's drive and a ferry ride south of Boston. He immediately said, "Oh, you have to visit us. You have to come over and spend some time with us." He lived there six to eight months of the year and spent the winter months in Florida.

For a moment, his eager invitation made me feel awkward. I didn't want him to feel obligated to invite us just because I had told him about our plans. But I'd spent a lot of time with him preparing for his class, and we had a good relationship. On the days he taught, he generally stayed overnight in the Kendall Hotel, which was basically on campus and only a couple blocks from the LGO offices. We often had dinner after class. Many times another student or two would join us, and I could see his sincere interest in them, their perspectives, and their lives. So, I immediately realized the invitation was pure Don—sincere, down to earth, a people guy, eager to meet my family. He invited us because he wanted us to come by.

When my family and I finally went to Martha's Vineyard, we found our way to his house in Chilmark, where he and his wife, Jinny, were expecting us.

Right away, he said, "Let me take you on a tour." As we walked around, he told us about the place, which I believe they had owned for decades, an old farm they'd converted to something of a country compound. Stanley Works, where he was CEO for a long time, was located in Connecticut, not far away on the mainland.

His two-story cottage was surrounded by grassy fields and set among huge beetlebung trees, which are indigenous to the island. Near the house was a barn with a hayloft where I think he said they once kept horses. By the time we saw it, the barn had become more of a workshop, with an old car in storage and a rope swing for kids.

On a nearby hill, maybe two hundred yards away, sat a huge, gorgeous house with a lovely view. I thought at first it was a neighbor's house until Don said, "That was our original family vacation home. As our family grew with grandkids, Jinny and I had the lower house built for us so that there would be plenty of room in the upper house for the growing families."

I thought, *Wow! How great!* He obviously built the house because he wanted to have his family close. He wanted them to feel comfortable coming and having their own space while still being part of their parent's life on the Vineyard.

It was a beautiful, late-spring day, sunny and warm. When we returned from the tour, we sat on the back patio and had lemonade, toast, butter, and jelly. I was struck by that because it seemed like an unusual snack. To Don though, it was perfectly normal.

We talked about kids and grandkids. Don said having our children there reminded him of when his grandchildren were little and they would come to visit. He and his wife had many memories of those times. He made me feel like I was visiting my grandparents' house, not the house of a CEO or a professor or someone else of his stature.

Then he took us into the house itself and showed us around. It was a real country home—floral wallpaper, big comfortable furniture, nothing modern, and a big homey country kitchen with lots of knickknacks and white cabinets with glass doors. The front hall was riddled with tennis rackets, balls, and fishing gear. Down one of the halls, Don had a private office with a TV and a big chair where he worked.

That's when he said, "I don't know if you know I write books." I didn't know, but I wouldn't have been surprised to learn that a successful CEO like Don had decided his long experience was worthy of writing a book, perhaps on leadership or how to have success in your business.

He asked his wife to find a copy, which she did, apparently the only copy they had. It was a children's book about a family of seagulls living on Martha's Vineyard.

I can still see the scene. Don took the book to a big, overstuffed, floral-print chair and ottoman in a sitting area off the kitchen. He sat there with my two kids nestled beside him as he read to them, just like your grandfather would read to you. The story, *Little Streak-Wing's Vineyard Adventure*, was about a family of seagulls who made their home on Martha's Vineyard and their adventures and all they see and do on the island, along with some important life lessons. Not surprisingly, Don had found a way to teach life lessons to children through the lives of the seagulls. He'd given all the seagulls names, and I think some of the names had some significance to his grandkids. He wrote it for them as a way to remember the Vineyard and the many things they did there.

It surprised me. I never imagined he would write a children's book.

When he finished, he said to my children, "I want you to have this book." I didn't want to take it because it was his only copy. But he insisted, saying, "I can get more printed, but I really want you to take it to remember your trip to Martha's Vineyard." He signed it and gave it to the kids.

We spent two or three hours there, enjoying the afternoon together, talking about family and life. He talked about his kids and some of the things he'd done at Stanley. It was a great experience for me, because I'd seen so much of him in and around the classroom, and this was a different setting and a different way of seeing him.

That day made as big an impression on me as anything I saw or heard in his class—maybe even bigger. It's made a difference in my life since.

For the past two and a half years, I served as the chief of staff for the vice chairman of a high-tech company who is responsible for running a large part of the organization. It was a pretty broad job, and I was regularly afforded opportunities to witness leadership in a variety of capacities. My work gave me a lot of exposure to and interaction with senior executives in the company, and I had the opportunity to lead and be involved in discussions that covered everything from strategy to important tactical issues. The job was a demanding one, but had many rewards including engaging in key decision-making, developing strategy, prioritizing financial objectives, preparing for discussions with customers, and creating communications for a global organization.

Don, with his mantras and, above all, his example, gave me a way to evaluate what I saw, to learn from everything around me, and a way to manage a busy and, at times, stressful work life. I was always asking myself, *How would Don have perceived that action or that comment?* Or, *What would Don have done in that situation?* I thought about those things because I was exposed to what I think Don was exposed to in his work— from board-of-directors meetings to the issues and problems faced by an executive leadership team on a day-to-day basis.

During my time in that job, as I remembered Don and observed the senior leaders I worked with and thought about my own aspirations, I became much more attuned to the successful leadership styles and characteristics of people I think are the most successful in the eyes of their people and the broader organization. More importantly, it was an education in that no one way proved to be the best. However, I've observed that leaders who are true to their own styles and beliefs and are committed to them in the face of adversity often get the greatest respect and the most effort from their teams—just as Don taught in his class.

I especially think about Don's life as a whole, not only his work but the time he had for family and the importance he attached to health and fitness.

Seeing Don and his life on Martha's Vineyard made me realize that you can be successful and still have balance. It was an "aha!" moment. I'd heard him talk in the classroom about the importance of balance, and I'd heard him talk about playing squash and tennis and the importance of staying fit. But in our visit I could actually see what he meant in his own life. This was a person, in my opinion, who had done it the right way, who was successful, who had had longevity in his career at the highest level, which isn't common in one company, and who had a wonderful family life—his kids and grandkids obviously adored him and loved to visit. This was the kind of guy you could use as a model, someone who, when they left this earth, would leave a legacy in so many different ways.

I've always tried to have good balance in my life, but my current job has made me be more conscious about it. I've made sure to spend more time with my family, especially because I have three children now. I've just completed my fourth marathon since leaving MIT in 2008. I'm a deacon at our church. I coach basketball and am active in Boy Scouts with my son. I taxi my daughter to soccer, play golf and basketball regularly, travel with my family, read, and enjoy a dinner club we have with friends.

I'm constantly seeking the balance Don had. It's easy to say I would do all these things without his encouragement. But, without what I learned from him, without his example and especially what I saw of his personal life on the Vineyard, I'm not sure. Seeing and hearing how he approached both life and work has been an enduring influence, and I'm grateful for it.

About MIT Leaders for Global Operations

The Leaders for Global Operations (LGO) program was launched in 1988 as Leaders for Manufacturing (LFM), a collaboration among the MIT Sloan School, the MIT School of Engineering, and a group of industry partners. During the era of "Made in America," with US manufacturing industries under threat by international competitors, LFM was created to align MIT's priorities with those of US industries and create a new source of leadership talent with management expertise and technical depth. In the twenty-seven years since its inception, the program's core partnership has endured, with several original industrial supporters now joined by a vibrant, international group of major global manufacturing and operations companies.

The program was renamed in 2009 as Leaders for Global Operations in order to recognize the changed reality of the manufacturing and operations world in which our partners operate and to which our graduates contribute as globally aware industrial leaders. The LFM founders referred to "big M manufacturing" as opposed to *just* the factory floor, recognizing that optimizing operations requires optimizing the entire enterprise. A well-honed plant surrounded by an unpredictable, high-latency supply chain, poor product development, or insufficient financial analysis and controls cannot excel. The "plants" that have been improved by LGO graduates include not only traditional manufacturing and assembly facilities but also hospitals, resorts, fulfillment centers, depots, government services, data centers, and nonprofit programs.

About Don Davis (1921-2010)

Donald W. Davis was the retired chairman and CEO of The Stanley Works. He began his business career in 1948 with Stanley and served in various line and staff positions before becoming executive vice president in 1962 and CEO in 1966. Under his leadership, Stanley grew to become a Fortune 500 company with annual sales approaching $2 billion.

Mr. Davis was past chairman of each of the following organizations: the National Association of Manufacturers, the Connecticut Business and Industry Association, the National Institute for Dispute Resolution, and the New Britain Connecticut Board of Education. At various times, Mr. Davis served as director for companies including Allied Signal Corp., Pitney Bowes, Connecticut Mutual Life Insurance Company, and the Dexter Manufacturing Company. After retiring from Stanley, he was a partner of American Industrial Partners, an investment company.

His proudest career achievement was becoming a senior lecturer at MIT's dual master's degree program, Leaders for Global Operations (LGO), where for twenty years he taught a class in leadership and ethics in business.

Not-for-profit boards on which Mr. Davis served included Martha's Vineyard Preservation Trust, Martha's Vineyard Hospital, and the Maya Angelou Public Charter School, Washington, DC.

Mr. Davis, a graduate of Penn State University, received his MBA from Harvard Business School. A naval officer during World War II, Mr. Davis was married to the former Virginia Cooper, with whom he shared six children and twelve grandchildren. Mr. and Mrs. Davis resided in Hobe Sound, Florida, and Chilmark, Massachusetts.

About the Editors

Stephen Cook

Stephen Cook is the executive managing director and cofounder of LFM Capital, a lower middle-market private equity fund focused on investing in niche US manufacturing companies. Steve is passionate about developing leadership teams at US manufacturing companies with high growth prospects. Before LFM Capital, he was a principal with TVV Capital. Previously, he was the COO for MFG.com, the world's largest global online marketplace for the manufacturing industry. He was also the director of consumer sales and Nashville site lead for Dell, where he managed a $1 billion P&L. He also was the director of manufacturing operations for Dell's Nashville campus, leading Dell's largest manufacturing plant in the world. In addition, he held executive positions with Dell in Austin, helping to start up two manufacturing plants and leading a team that redesigned Dell's global inbound supply chain. Stephen is a 1998 graduate of the Leaders for Global Operations program at MIT, where he earned an MBA and SM in electrical engineering and computer science and graduated at the top of his class. He also has a BS in electrical engineering from the US Naval Academy. Prior to attending MIT, he flew A-6 Intruders from the USS *America* in Iraq, Bosnia, and Somalia. He also flew all US Navy/Marine Corps tactical aircraft in a test squadron.

Ruthie Davis

Ruthie Davis, founder, chief executive officer and designer of her eponymous label, is a world-renowned global luxury footwear designer. She earned her bachelor's degree in English and visual arts at Bowdoin College and her MBA in entrepreneurship from Babson's Olin Graduate School of Business. Ruthie held senior executive positions in design and marketing at Reebok, UGG Australia, and Tommy Hilfiger before launching RUTHIE DAVIS in 2006. Her brand is sold in high-end retailers worldwide, including Neiman Marcus, Bergdorf Goodman, Bloomingdale's, Harvey Nichols, and Amazon. RUTHIE DAVIS shoes are a top choice of A-list celebrities such as Beyoncé, Lady Gaga, Jennifer Lopez, Kim Kardashian, and Halle Berry. Ruthie was named the 2014 Footwear Designer of the Year by the American Apparel & Footwear Association, one of Goldman Sachs's 100 Most Intriguing Entrepreneurs in 2013, and one of *Footwear News'* Directional Design Stars in 2013 & 2014. In 2014 Ruthie Davis was the only footwear designer to be accepted into the CFDA (Council of Fashion Designers of America). In 2015, she received Babson's Alumni Entrepreneur Hall of Fame Award. Ruthie is the youngest daughter of Virginia and Don Davis, and Don was her mentor, role model, and inspiration in both business and life. She lives in the West Chelsea district of New York City with her husband, Innes Weir, and three Italian greyhounds, Desert, River and Sky.

Carol Franco

Carol Franco became an affiliated agent with Kneerim, Williams & Bloom literary agency in 2005, specializing in business and general non-fiction. Now a resident of Santa Fe, Carol was a publishing executive in Boston for more than twenty-five years. As director, she led the Harvard Business School Press to a position of market leadership, signing many of the Press's most distinguished and successful authors such as Michael Porter, John Kotter, Gary Hamel, C. K. Prahalad, Warren Bennis, and Charles Handy. Prior to Harvard, she was president of Ballinger

Publishing, where she created a line of influential business books that became the foundation for HarperBusiness, a subsidiary of HarperCollins. She is also the coauthor, with Kent Lineback, of *The Legacy Guide: Capturing the Facts, Memories, and Meaning of Your Life*, published by Tarcher/Penguin in January 2007.

Kent Lineback

Kent Lineback coaches and helps executives and companies tell their stories so that others can learn from their experiences. He has authored, coauthored, or collaborated with business leaders and thinkers on fifteen books, including two best sellers. He has coauthored four *Harvard Business Review* articles, as well as pieces in other business journals, such as the *European Business Review*, and blogs for harvardbusiness.org, fortune.com, *Huffington Post*, and IBM. With Linda Hill, a professor at Harvard Business School, he has coauthored two books: *Collective Genius: The Art and Practice of Leading Innovation* (Harvard Business Review Press, 2014) and *Being the Boss: The 3 Imperatives for Becoming a Great Leader* (Harvard Business Press, 2011), a best seller that reviewers hailed as a "modern management classic" and "the manager's bible." Prior to his current work as a writer and coach, he spent over twenty-five years as a leader and executive in private, public, not-for-profit, and governmental organizations. He holds a BA from Harvard College and an MBA from Boston College.

Dan Shockley

Dan Shockley is an experienced manufacturing executive with a passion for leadership development. He is currently a managing director and cofounder at LFM Capital, a lower middle-market private equity firm based in Nashville. LFM Capital is passionate about boosting the US manufacturing renaissance by investing in and growing niche US manufacturing companies. LFM is focused on partnering with and developing great leadership teams in its portfolio companies to catalyze change and improvement. Prior to LFM Capital, Dan was the general manager of Ditch Witch, a family-owned business that has been a leader in underground construction equipment. Before Ditch Witch, Dan held various leadership roles at Caterpillar, including general manager for the remanufacturing business in Europe, Africa, and the Middle East, as well as plant manager for a start-up remanufacturing facility in Shanghai. Dan earned an SM in mechanical engineering and an MBA from MIT, where he attended the Leaders for Global Operations program. He also received a BS in metallurgical engineering from the Missouri University of Science and Technology.

Jonathan Strimling

Jonathan Strimling is a seasoned executive and entrepreneur, currently serving as chief executive officer of SMTP Inc., a global provider of e-mail–related services. Within six months of his arrival at SMTP, he helped propel the company to the NASDAQ via a highly successful public offering. Previously, Mr. Strimling cofounded three successful businesses in the renewable-energy industry—WoodPellets.com, US Dynamics, and UltraCell Insulation—which have already displaced hundreds of millions of pounds of carbon emissions. Mr. Strimling previously served in a variety of leadership roles with American Industrial Partners, General Electric, and DEKA Research and Development. Mr. Strimling has served on the boards of the Biomass Thermal Energy Council, the Alliance for Green Heat, and was appointed by New Hampshire's Governor Lynch to the state's Economic Strategy Commission. Mr. Strimling earned two master's degrees in management and engineering from MIT's Sloan School of Management and holds a bachelor's degree in mechanical engineering from Northeastern University. Mr. Strimling is a third-generation entrepreneur with two young children that he is hoping will also be able to enjoy and benefit from Don Davis's lessons in leadership.

Jeff Wilke

Jeff Wilke is currently the senior vice president, consumer business at Amazon.com. Jeff's direct reports include the business leaders for Amazon's North American retail websites, plus the global leaders of operations, technology, marketing, Prime, and third-party seller services, who support Amazon's global consumer businesses. Jeff joined Amazon.com in 1999 as VP of worldwide operations. Jeff left AlliedSignal (now Honeywell), where he was vice president and general manager of pharmaceutical fine chemicals. Jeff spent the preceding six years in a variety of operations and general management assignments in the chemical, polymer, and electronics industries. Jeff is a 1993 graduate of MIT's Leaders for Global Operations program, where he earned an MBA and an SM in chemical engineering. He began his working career writing code and managing software development projects at Andersen Consulting (now Accenture). He also holds a BSE degree in chemical engineering, summa cum laude, from Princeton University. Jeff serves as the chairman of the governing board for MIT's Leaders for Global Operations program, as a member of the dean's advisory council for Princeton University's School of Engineering and Applied Science, and as a board member of Code.org. He lives with his family in Seattle, Washington, and was born and raised in Pittsburgh, Pennsylvania.

Made in the USA
San Bernardino, CA
06 November 2015